NOTHING NEW

ALSO BY ROBYN ANNEAR

Bearbrass

Nothing but Gold

The Man Who Lost Himself

Fly a Rebel Flag

A City Lost and Found

ROBYN ANNEAR

NOTHING NEW

A HISTORY OF SECOND-HAND

TEXT PUBLISHING MELBOURNE AUSTRALIA

textpublishing.com.au

The Text Publishing Company
Swann House, 22 William Street, Melbourne Victoria 3000, Australia

Published by The Text Publishing Company, 2019

Book design by Imogen Stubbs
Cover images from iStock
Typeset in Adobe Garamond Pro 12.25/17.5 by J&M Typesetting

Printed and bound in Australia by Griffin Press, part of Ovato, an accredited ISO/NZS 14001:2004 Environmental Management System printer

ISBN: 9781922268303 (hardback)
ISBN: 9781925923018 (ebook)

A catalogue record for this book is available from the National Library of Australia

This book is printed on paper certified against the Forest Stewardship Council® Standards. Griffin Press holds FSC chain-of-custody certification SGS-COC-005088. FSC promotes environmentally responsible, socially beneficial and economically viable management of the world's forests.

For Val Annear, my brilliant mum.

When one sees a crowd of ill-clad women with suit cases and sugar bags wending their way in subdued excitement to a hall in the afternoon one may be pretty certain that a jumble sale is there.

AGE (MELBOURNE), 1924

CONTENTS

Introduction

One little flapper beamed with delight when she became the possessor of a pair of silver shoes for sixpence.

HERALD (MELBOURNE), DECEMBER 1925

Millie Tallis came up with the idea.

It was the winter of 1925 and St Vincent's Hospital was looking to expand. A fundraising appeal was launched, headed by Melbourne's lord mayor and a committee of worthies that included Sir George Tallis. Sir George had made his fortune as a theatrical impresario and his good lady wife—before she *was* his wife, of course—had starred, in tights and satin bloomers, as a comic-opera 'gem'. Now the pair shone bright in the constellation of Melbourne society.

Over the course of several months, raffles were held and balls mounted; there was a car rally, a beauty contest, a telephone girls' carnival, a brass-band extravaganza—the usual things. Also usual would have been a jumble sale, held over one or two days in a hall with room enough for trestle tables and the serving of tea. But the St Vincent's committee had at its disposal something better than just any old hall: on the site of the hospital's proposed expansion stood the Cyclorama.

Forty metres in diameter, with a high, domed roof, the Cyclorama was built in 1889 to house a 360-degree painted panorama, which audiences viewed from a central platform. It's hard now to imagine how the Cyclorama ever rated as much of a thrill; the panorama, depicting one bloody tumult or another—the Battle of Waterloo, Eureka Stockade, the Siege of Paris—was changed only every few years. In any case, early in the new century, moving pictures had made a white elephant of the whole thing. What use then was there for a circular building, even (or especially) one surmounted with the crenellated façade of a castle? Other than as a pigeon loft, it served fitfully as a boxing stadium and as storage for stage props, then St Vincent's acquired it with a view to demolition.

Lady Tallis and her husband had just returned from a motoring tour that took them through France and across the US, where they'd witnessed the popularity of second-hand shops run on charitable lines. Why not try something similar in aid of St Vincent's—a shop, rather than a jumble sale? Lady Tallis took charge and, in christening the enterprise, paid a nod to its continental progenitor, *le magasin d'occasion*. But while the French *occasion* here signifies 'bargain', it can also be used to mean 'opportunity'. Did Lady Tallis mistranslate, or was it a knowing distinction she made—or even a small cross-lingual pun? Whichever, it came to pass that, for three months straddling Christmas 1925, the Cyclorama played host to the first ever opportunity shop.

ᔕ

Other people's detritus *calls* to me. And from that siren song this book was born.

Op shops being my element, my first thought was to trace their origins, which led me to Lady Tallis and the bargain shops of interwar France. But second-handing, it turns out, stretches back and back across millennia. Common sense dictates that *used* must always have followed *new*. The archaic word *handsel*, denoting the first sale or use of a thing, posits the inevitability of successive sale or use. Innovation, kinship, trade, status, crime, migration, fashion, death—all have been timeless generators of second-hand.

In the dictionary, second-hand keeps company with

second-best and *second-rate*—and *second thoughts*: consider the lyrebird's repertoire. Certain historians have identified with Baudelaire's portrait of the *chiffonier*, or urban scavenger, who sorted through 'everything that the big city has cast off, everything it lost, everything it disdained, everything it broke'. And if few intellectuals would embrace Friedrich Hayek's definition of them as 'second-hand dealers in ideas', not many would refute it either.*

Given the way we live now, it would be easy to suppose that newness has always been venerated. But such a notion was almost unknown until late in the eighteenth century, and gained wide currency only during the twentieth. With the advent of consumerism, obsolescence supplanted re-use in the life cycle of things. Of course, second-hand goods didn't cease to exist but, with the exception of cars, the no-longer-new lost its value and was disregarded. Not just used but used up.

The second-hand industry has drawn the attention of academics in disciplines ranging from economics and marketing to fashion and textiles, history and sociology. Most seem to have approached the subject ethnographically, as observers of a repellent custom. As recently as 2015, one British academic—a geographer and social researcher—wrote that 'the purchasing of pre-consumed

* Hayek himself, undeniably an original thinker, blueprinted a supercharged engine for inequality: the free market.

used clothing…is perceived negatively as undesirable'. Good grief—now he tells me.

My mum had no sisters, only girl cousins who were just her age and size, which pretty much ruled out hand-me-downs. But, Depression and war-time privation notwithstanding, her mother contrived to keep her smartly dressed. Not being one of nature's needlewomen, Gran outfitted her little girl in quality second-hand from market stalls that promised their stock came exclusively from homes in the 'better' suburbs.

If Mum had no problem with second-hand, Dad surely did. Thanks to a stiff-necked upbringing, he was rigid about many—to be honest, most—things. He'd been raised alone by his mother, whom department stores employed to inflict the cruel art of corset-fitting, and who impressed on her boy that only new was good enough. No second-hand for us, then.

Not that second-hand was really an option in the sixties and seventies, unless you were a charity case. Ours being a fissile nuclear family, cousins didn't feature, and even if they had, Dad's standards would have ruled their (or anybody's) cast-offs unwelcome. But new clothes were pricey and money was tight. Luckily Mum had trained as a dressmaker: equipped with a sewing machine and no end of resourcefulness, she kept us decently, if not fashionably, clad.

It was my further luck to come of age just as suburban opportunity shops began to proliferate. Doubtless, too, I was influenced by the example of my mum's thrift and ingenuity, as well as by a kind of furtive rebelliousness that stirred in her as Dad retreated from family life. (And hey, it was the seventies.) I can't now recall my first visit to our local op shop—I'd guess it was 1976—but Mum would have been with me, for sure. And that counted as having the blessing of my idol.*

The following year I changed schools. Life up till then had confined me to the burgeoning suburb of Doncaster, a former orcharding district subdivided into quarter-acres and planted with brick veneers—twelve miles by bus from the centre of Melbourne. Now, for my final year of school, I switched to a college in the CBD. Most of the other students were aged in their twenties or older, returning to study so as to qualify for a free university education. I was a young sixteen. I knew by heart every song by Rodgers and Hammerstein and not one of the Rolling Stones'.

That year was, let's say, an eye-opener. Besides discovering the possibilities of the adult world, I began to glean hints of my own character. The temptations set before me were three: sex, drugs and second-hand.

There was a shop in Swanston Street that sold smokers'

* When I asked her recently about her history with op shops, Mum insisted that it was *me* who introduced *her* to them.

paraphernalia, incense, Indian skirts smelling of jute, T-shirts printed with profanities and, upstairs, racks of vintage clothing. I have a recollection (smoke-hazed) of floaty, bias-cut, nipped-waist and knife-pleated garments dating from the 1920s to the '50s. I liked to look and linger, but the prices were beyond me.

No, I found my thrill in Box Hill: at the jumble sale that ran three days each week in a hall attached to the Salvation Army citadel. The hall was packed, but not with shoppers; often I was the only one there. There were racks and shelves and trestle tables, all crammed to overflowing with old stuff. *Seriously* old stuff, representing a lifetime's accumulation by people just getting to dying age, people who had tended to keep things rather than throw them away.

The stock sorting at the Salvos' jumble sale was rudimentary: clothes separated from books; white elephants just anywhere. But an hour or two of dedicated searching never failed to turn up treasure. Treasure to me, anyway. My vividest jumble-sale memory is of squirrelling beneath one of the trestle tables, where a rolled-up bedspread and a stack of wire desk trays concealed a square brown case. The lid, relieved of its overburden, rose of its own volition—and a head appeared! It belonged to a spring-loaded resuscitation dummy (head and torso only) with matinee-idol looks and implacably waved rubber hair.

Liberated from his leatherette sepulchre Lionel, as he was henceforth known, would raise (or, anyway, set) the tone of half a dozen share houses over the next decade.

Nothing at the jumble sale carried a price tag. The drill was to select as much stuff as you could carry, then submit to the benevolence of the lady volunteers who kept the cash tin at a table by the door. (Always the same two, they had a good-cop/bad-cop thing going.) Second only to Lionel in my pantheon of memorable finds were two 1930s evening gowns—from the back of the same wardrobe, I'd wager: one of slinky gold lace lined in silk, with a cabochon-clasp belt; the other of beaded dusky-pink crepe, with a sweeping train and bolero jacket. Adjudged 'something special', they cost me two dollars apiece.

These few recollected highlights of the Box Hill Salvos' jumble sale contain the gist of what I find irresistible about old stuff and the finding of it. Serendipity. Never knowing what you'll find. Sometimes nothing, sometimes gold; most often, fool's gold. Expectations are worthless when op-shopping, and so it is the perfect sport for a glass-half-empty person like me. I love the gonzo X factor, the inscrutable hints of past lives, the bargains.

Not long ago in our local Salvos', I picked up, for ten dollars, an English-made 1960s wool and mohair coat of emerald green, lined with matching satin. I had dreamed (or, to be honest, daydreamed) of finding a coat that colour. Hanging at the end of the rack, it must have just been put into stock. Ten minutes later—five, even—and it would have been gone. Surely that emerald-green coat and I were meant for each other. We had, it seemed to me, a reciprocal bond: luck had blessed me with my dream-coat, and this (frankly) old coat had been blessed with my stewardship. Notwithstanding my heedlessness of wardrobe moths, the emerald-green coat will be treasured and worn with joy.

For me, at sixteen and still today, second-hand has been a means of self-invention, a haphazard route to a haphazard personal style. Its variety, its unpredictability, allow me to be playful, trying things on in a way that straight-up fashion seeks to undermine and control.

ও

Second-hand means different things to different people. To some it's an abhorrence, to some a necessity, to others a curiosity, a business, an aesthetic, an obsession, a mode of time-travel. It is all but ineradicable: things don't just disappear because our use for them has ended. In *Lady Oracle,* an early novel of Margaret Atwood's, the protagonist observes of London's Portobello Road market how—

> *The people died but their possessions did not, they went around and around as in a slow eddy...How difficult these objects are to dispose of, I thought.*

Even 'the costliest garments, the bravest panoplies' must eventually wash up as cast-offs. Where inequality exists—that is, everywhere and always—second-hand trickles down, variously bestowing insult, comfort, and delight. Many can afford used goods of quality and prestige that, when new, would have been beyond their means. But second-hand doesn't create equality and won't overturn global capitalism—is, in fact, a by-product of it: a species of waste.

Although there's more second-hand in circulation than ever, you'll often hear the lament that 'all the good stuff's gone now'. Since at least the 1850s, dealers and devotees have pined for a lost golden age of second-hand, always twenty years in the past, when every shop and market stall offered treasures of a kind now confined to the museum or auction catalogue. Or on eBay which, nowadays, has made a dead letter of serendipity. Anything you could possibly want is there, just keystrokes away. Which is fine if you're after a particular thing—if finding, rather than seeking, is the point.

But give me ten minutes in an op shop and see if I can't turn up something I didn't know I was looking for: red Giddy Gams pantyhose (circa 1971), still in their cellophane packet; a cracked school slate, the exact dimensions of an iPad; a book of short stories printed entirely in Pitman's shorthand; a pair of men's patent leather dress shoes with pages of a 1952 newspaper stuffed into the toes.

Nothing New traces the history of second-hand in all its questionable morality, legality and hygiene. The purpose of this introduction has been to alert you, dear reader, to…let's call it my bias. Second-hand is manna to me.

CHAPTER I

Nothing New

There's nothing new about second-hand. For most of history people have lived with scarcity. A finite number of things to go round meant that the inelastic fabric-of-stuff had to be made to stretch and, as populations grew and hierarchies hardened, the fabric wore thinnest at the edges.

We hear of people dressed in rags; but rags, like dust, exist in the eye of the beholder. A rag isn't a rag while it can still be worn. In the past, all things had long lives—used, re-used, refashioned—that tapered into afterlives as constituents of other things. Exchange, for the longest time, was most people's currency. Things—clothing, tools, furniture, bedding—changed hands by gift or inheritance, by barter, loan, wager or theft. Or by sale; but in pre-industrial society, except among the elite, that would have been the least usual mode of exchange.

Clothing was at the heart of the trade in second-hand. Ordinary people's lives being uninflected by fashion cycles, clothing that had served one generation served the next just as well. Alteration and mending to extend the life of garments were no small part of a woman's work. And of the goods that circulated second-hand, none was more indispensable than clothing: custom, if not climate, dictated that even a homeless beggar must have the bare minimum to stand up in.

The Bible tells of how, after the crucifixion, Jesus's clothes were divided, as per custom, between the soldiers on the spot. They drew lots for His robe and the girdle that tied it, His head-dress, sandals and under-tunic. These weren't souvenirs but a perk (short for perquisite), or entitlement, which the soldiers would have counted on to sell or barter. At His resurrection, Jesus was mistaken by Mary Magdalene for a gardener and some have surmised that, rising naked from the tomb, He may have borrowed clothes from a gravedigger's hut close at hand.

The belongings of regular people would have

been distributed, after their death, among family and neighbours or else given as dues to creditors—or perhaps to the servant who had nursed and laid out the departed. A person's will might bequeath their 'best suit of apparel' to one family member and their 'wearing cloathes' to another. (Shakespeare famously left his 'second best bed' to his wife.) Bequests like these highlight the real, transferable value of everyday possessions when, for all but the topmost elite, there was a limited pool of stuff in circulation. Away from cities and towns large enough to have their makers and markets, even gentry might rely on local auctions of deceased estates to replenish their wardrobe or household goods. 'New' was commonly understood to mean not brand new but newly acquired.

In Britain towards the end of the eighteenth century, the cost of clothing consumed about ten per cent of an average family's income. Those living in towns were better placed than the rural poor to pick up a good second-hand coat or pair of boots (both major outlays, but essential) at between a quarter and a third the price of new. The value and longevity of clothing made it an investment that could be liquidated in hard times. Here, too, town-dwellers had the advantage of ready access to second-hand dealers, as well as to pawnbrokers or moneylenders who would accept any goods—clothing being the most common—as security on loans.

A major portion of any dealer's stock of second-hand clothing came from servants. Many, perhaps most, lower-class people spent some years 'in service' when young, and often would receive their employers' cast-offs as a perk, in addition to wages. At some periods and places there were conventions, and even laws, that inhibited a servant from wearing their master's old clothes. Ornate details or risqué styling might give offence or be socially misleading if worn by a person of the wrong class. Servants sometimes kept gifted clothing as a form of savings to be drawn on in later life, for sale or remaking in times of need. More often though, it would be sold straightaway.

The existence of regulating bodies (guilds or 'mysteries') of second-hand dealers in the cities of Europe as early as the thirteenth century suggests that the industry was well established even then. Members of the trade in London were known as upholders or upholsters, names that would come to specify dealers in second-hand furniture. Their clothes-broking brethren would splinter off as fripperers, a name borrowed from their French counterparts, the *fripiers* (or *fripières*), and having its origin in the word for 'rag'. By the eighteenth century, travelling dealers known simply as 'salesmen' traded in second-hand clothing between British towns and the countryside; a village store- or innkeeper might act as their local agent and depot. Tailors dealt in both new and used clothing, accepting second-hand in part-payment for new. In 1762, desperate for money to lavish on his paramour, the rakish James Boswell resorted to selling redundant items of apparel. He got eleven shillings for 'a suit of old clothes' and, for the lace from an old hat ('Off it went with my sharp penknife'), a jeweller in Piccadilly gave him six shillings and sixpence, 'which was a great cause of joy to me'.

Boswell might equally have taken his things to a pawnshop. For as long as there'd been notions of ownership and debt, borrowers had lodged portable items of value with moneylenders as security on loans: tools, weapons, jewellery, household goods, bedding and clothing—especially clothing. A warm coat might be pawned during summer months; a Sunday-best outfit would be hocked mid-week to put food on the table, then redeemed—the loan repaid, with interest—on Saturday payday. Items unclaimed were put up for sale by the pawnbroker, creating a steady source of cheap second-hand. But a pawnshop was a rarity outside of the cities until about the time Boswell was selling his suit. Their spread into the countryside formalised age-old ways of balancing a family budget and made the poor beholden to a man they spoke of as Uncle, a notional kinsman they could turn to in lean times.

For much of history, though, at the village and

neighbourhood level, the second-hand economy was run by women and relied mainly on barter and exchange of favours. A widow trusted to deliver babies and nurse the dying might also be known to her neighbours as a second-hand broker and moneylender. Such women had an intimate knowledge of their communities—who needed what, who was struggling, who was able to pay (or repay)—and could deal discreetly with other women at the crossroads of neighbourliness and opportunism. And, as makers, menders and launderers, women were the clothing specialists.

This informal second-hand trade might have eluded history's radar were it not for surviving records of criminal trials. Who was it that predominated, for centuries, as 'fences'—receivers of stolen property in exchange for ready cash? Widows, wives and spinsters, that's who. Among the first convicts to land at Sydney Cove in 1788 were Fanny Anderson and Dorothy Handland, both sent south for crimes related to clothes theft and both giving their occupation as 'old clothes woman'.* Sarah Burdo, a dressmaker transported in 1788, sold 'the worst of my clothes' on the voyage out, two petticoats and a long black coat that fetched a sum close to a labourer's annual earnings back home.

* Handland, reputedly the First Fleet's oldest convict, counted as a doubly-old clothes woman.

But, these glimpses notwithstanding, the best evidence for the ubiquity of second-hand in the pre-modern era is that it was so little mentioned—that is, it was so taken for granted and so (literally) off-the-books it left hardly a trace in the historical record. In Europe, second-hand persisted as the unremarked norm from antiquity until late in the eighteenth century, during which time industry lacked the capacity, or the demand, to produce new goods for everybody. 'Making do' was how people lived and all that they expected.

The eighteenth century didn't end with the turning of a calendar page, but overlapped the nineteenth to bracket the Enlightenment and the rise of the Industrial Revolution. Enlightenment ideas taking root in Europe from the mid-eighteenth century emphasised formal economies of trade and currency, and promoted progress through veneration of The New. Here was the birth of fashion, an aspirational standard* by which *new* meant not just new but *newest*, and obsolescence arrived by design. Fashion sped up the cycle of consumption and replacement, fuelling markets with the *wanting* of things.

Only then, when conspicuously new became fixed as the desirable norm, did second-hand come into focus as a distinct category, inferior by definition. The trade

* (a *paradigm* in all but name)

itself—shapeless, informal, run by those on the margins—was at odds with the new economic order. Second-hand was surely a foot-dragging aberration, the antithesis of progress and the enemy of new.

But still, for a long time, it was all that most people could afford. Unlike the usual contagions, fashion infected the high end first and took a while to get a grip on the masses. In Britain around 1800, it's thought, an annual family income of £50 would have been the threshold of active consumerism: of following fashion and buying new merchandise. The majority of families earned less than that amount and instead consumed the cast-offs of their betters.

As the nineteenth century gathered steam on rails laid by the Industrial Revolution, the ranks of active consumers would expand mightily. An upward shift in status became possible as never before, especially in the New World. Advances in processing, manufacturing and distribution made clothing much cheaper (furniture and household goods as well), and advertising and retailing scaled up to mechanise status and fashion at street-level. By the 1850s, not only the burgeoning middle class but those aspiring to join it could afford to dress in new, ready-made clothing, leaving second-hand to the very poorest.

Paradoxically, as newness became normal, so the

newly transgressive second-hand industry became a topic of social commentary. These were the early days of slum journalism, a form of reportage whereby those who qualified as active consumers were entertained and scandalised (mildly) by scenes of squalor among the lower ranks.

So it was that readers of the *Morning Chronicle* and *Household Words*, and of innumerable inky syndications from Bundaberg, Queensland, to Butte, Montana, would be shown along Petticoat Lane on a market day, or behind the counter of a pawnbroker's shop, or inside the basket on a street-vendor's back. These travellers' tales from the urban frontier captured the late blooming of an age-old industry, the vagaries of fashion having ensured a greater supply of *stuff* than ever before.

CHAPTER 2

Ol' Clo'

There are many parts of the metropolis which are as much unknown to the great majority of the population as are the unexplored localities at the antipodes...And yet there is not a scene in London more worthy of being witnessed than that which the Rag Fair exhibits.

JOURNALIST JAMES GRANT, 1842

'Rag Fair' meant Petticoat Lane, and 'Petticoat Lane' meant not just one single street but a web of offshoots with names like Tripe Yard and Catherine-wheel Alley that covered perhaps three meandering miles of Houndsditch, in London's east end. The district had grown up outside the old city wall and been settled, from the sixteenth century, by Jewish émigrés. Despite being outside the city proper, it became the centre of pawnbroking and second-hand dealing and host to Rag Fair.

There had always been a Rag Fair. Before Petticoat

Lane, it could be found in Birchover's Lane, right in the heart of the city. When the satirist Pope wrote, in 1728, of Rag Fair as 'a place near the Tower of London, where old cloaths and frippery are sold', it was Rosemary Lane he meant. Petticoat Lane market grew out of—and outgrew—Rosemary Lane, and the two, separated by little more than quarter of a mile, often shared the name Rag Fair. In the eighteenth century, Monmouth Street, Seven Dials, rivalled Petticoat Lane as the 'great mart for second-hand apparel'—so much so that the expression 'Monmouth Street finery' came to signify anything tawdry or sham. Writing for the *Morning Chronicle* in 1836, Charles Dickens called Monmouth Street 'the burial-place of fashions; and such, to judge from present appearances, it will remain until there are no more fashions to bury'. (That day has yet to come, but Monmouth Street is no longer the boneyard.)

These were street markets in the most literal sense: their merchandise was arrayed and displayed on the street itself, spread out or piled up 'on wrappers, or pieces of matting or carpet'. Dresses might be bundled up on the ground, slung in layers over chairs, or hung from doorways and window frames fronting the street.

> *Petticoat-lane proper is long and narrow* [wrote the journalist and social researcher Henry Mayhew], *and to look down it is to look down a*

vista of many coloured garments, alike on the sides and on the ground...it is a vista of dinginess, but many coloured dinginess, as regards female attire.

In men's clothing, black and dark blue predominated. Boots and shoes were heaped up or laid out in rows, hats stacked in unsteady towers. And it wasn't just apparel that was spread out for sale, but anything and everything 'from a wooden leg to an orrery'. Haggling was not just allowed but expected, and a customer who did it right would end up paying perhaps a quarter of the price first asked. With its 'narrow streets, dark alleys, and most oppressive crowding', clamorous with street cries and hard bargaining, Petticoat Lane in the 1850s presented a scene, said Mayhew, 'which cannot be beheld in any other part of the greatest city in the world, nor in any other portion of the world itself'. (By way of comparison, he'd been to Paris and Calcutta.)

Speculation as to the romance of a garment's past lives was an invariable feature of any journalistic treatment of the second-hand trade.

We love to walk among these extensive groves of the illustrious dead, and to indulge in the speculations to which they give rise; now fitting a deceased coat, then a pair of trousers, and anon the mortal remains of a gaudy waistcoat, upon some being of our own conjuring up, and endeavouring, from the shape and fashion of the garment itself, to bring its former owner before our mind's eye.

This was Dickens's 'Meditations in Monmouth-Street'—so we can well believe in his 'conjuring up' a character from a few shreds of old clobber. Mostly, though, such reveries ('how many privations have been endured before some of these habiliments found their way into the possession of the old-clothes man…') smack of the hyperbole and bathos that were the stamp of slum journalism. The writers were writing as tourists: in the market for colour and novelty. Actual shoppers at the street stalls would have been alert not to a garment's genealogy but to the immediate possibilities of fit and fabric and the all-important question of price.

London's second-hand trade had greatly expanded since the late eighteenth century. In 1833 there were reckoned to be ten thousand second-hand clothes sellers in London, where there'd been three hundred or so half a century earlier. That proliferation was attributed to servants selling on the 'many cast-off clothes allowed them, through the increased extravagance of their masters'. And coinciding with the surplus born of consumerism was a surge of Jewish immigrants. Urban in origin and fleeing oppression, they were resourceful in the ways needed to make a living from second-hand. Many of them were expert in tailoring and bootmaking, able to add value to even the tattiest of cast-offs. Besides, finding employment outside their community was hard, since the usual six-day working week included Saturday, the Jewish *Shabbat*.

The sprawling mass of street-sellers and shopfronts on Monmouth Street or along Petticoat Lane and its tributaries was only the retail face of the London second-hand trade. Any servant wishing to convert their perks into cash or householders with cast-offs to sell wouldn't have carried the goods to Rag Fair. No, the buyers came to them. The roving old-clothes man (or woman, sometimes) was a fixture of any urban neighbourhood; a city like London had hundreds of them. Each had his territory, or 'walk', of which he daily traversed 'every street, square and road, with the monotonous cry, sometimes like a bleat, of "Clo'! Clo'!"'—so that he and his brethren were known as ol' clo' men.

If the old-clothes buyers were mostly men, those they bought from were nearly always women. Servants at the kitchen door, mistresses at the front. Henry Mayhew, who inventoried London's 'street-folk' in the 1850s, conducted interviews with several in the ol' clo' line. Most bought whatever garments were on offer, but there were those who specialised, like this buyer of 'gentlemen's left-off wearing apparel'—

> *They are either the wives of tradesmen or mechanics who sell them to us, or else it is the servant of a lodging-house, who has had the things given to her…She comes to 'em light, and of course she parts with 'em light…But the mistresses of the houses are she-dragons.* [Hard bargainers, he meant.] *Many a time they sells their husband's things unbeknown to 'e, and often the gentleman of the house coming up to the door, and seeing us make a deal—for his trowsers maybe—puts a stop to the whole transaction.*

In streets near the docks, there were always sailors' clothes to be bought from women with whom seamen lodged or consorted when ashore.* And, contrary to what you might imagine, Mayhew found that the poorer the neighbourhood, the more clothing was offered for sale.

Ol' clo' buyers who lacked a ready purse of cash might coax 'a man's third-best coat from his good lady at home' by offering in exchange new crockery and glassware or even, at certain seasons, blooming fuchsias and geraniums.† These traders were perpetuating the old cashless economy that enabled women, in particular, to upgrade

* Dickens wrote: 'A sailor generally pawns or sells all he has before he has been long ashore, and if he does not, some favoured companion kindly saves him the trouble.'

† This mode of exchange would persist into the twentieth century: a worn top hat, in Liverpool around 1905, was worth one aspidistra.

old possessions for new. One 'crock-barterer' outlined for Mayhew his rates of exchange—

> *A good tea-service we generally give for a left-off suit of clothes, hat and boots—they must all be in a decent condition to be worth that. We give a sugar-basin for an old coat, and a rummer* [drinking glass] *for a pair of old Wellington boots. For a glass milk-jug I should expect a waistcoat and trowsers, and they must be tidy ones too.*

The barterer would head off at daybreak with a basketful of crockery and glass, touting their wares through the streets with the ambiguous cry of 'Clo'! Old clo'!' To anyone asking the price of an item, their answer would be, 'Have you got any old clothes?' This was the age of whatnots, antimacassars and knick-knackery; no surface was suffered to go bare. 'Often and often,' a trader told Mayhew, 'I've known a woman sell the best part of her husband's stock of clothes for china ornaments for her mantelpiece.' In the course of a day, the huckster might walk twenty-five kilometres or more with an unwieldy load, 'for as fast as I gets rid on [*sic*] the weight of the crockery, I takes up the weight of the old clothes'. A good day might see him return home carrying—

> *...a bundle of old clothes, consisting of two or three old shirts, a coat or two, a suit of left-off livery, a woman's gown may be, or a pair of old stays, a*

couple of pair of Wellingtons, and a waistcoat or so. These I should have at my back, and the remainder of my china and glass on my head, and very probably an umbrella or two under my arm, and five or six old hats in my hand.

Around the same time, householders in small-town America were warned against 'a certain class' of travelling peddlers who offered parlour ornaments and Bohemian glass in exchange for cast-off clothing. Let them in and they'd fleece you, was the gist. Settlers in remote parts of Australia relied, for staples as well as luxuries, on periodic calls by Chinese and Indian hawkers for whom second-hand goods—at least in part-exchange—were an acceptable currency long after shops insisted on cash.

If you lived in the English countryside, you might open your door in the dead of winter to find a 'shallow-cove', nearly naked, pleading for old clothes to cover his gooseflesh and his shame. Or a barefoot 'limper', begging for boots. Trading sob-stories (the 'shipwrecked sailor' routine was a staple) for cast-offs, a roaming band of beggars might thus accumulate a stock of second-hand apparel to sell or barter at the next market town they came to.

For much of their history, London's open-air markets dealt in wholesale as well as retail, buying off ol' clo' men and crock-barterers and selling on to the trade as well as to individual customers. That changed in 1843, when the Old Clothes Exchange was founded close by Petticoat Lane. The city had its stock exchange and the Royal Exchange, as well as exchanges for the trading of commodities like grain, coal and textiles; and the great markets of Smithfield (cattle), Billingsgate (fish) and Covent Garden (flowers, fruit and vegetables) were the wholesale exchanges for fresh produce. Why not a clearing house for old clothes?

In reality, the Old Clothes Exchange was a response—as, doubtless, had been others of those commodity exchanges—to official pressure aimed at bringing order to an ungovernable trade. The traditional ad hoc-ery of street-trading didn't fit well with the values of the changing urban economy. Street markets defied regulation, hindered traffic, and were an (admittedly entertaining) eyesore. As commercial life in London assumed a more formal character, market traders came under pressure to shift their business indoors. This was how, as other street markets were cleaned up and closed down, the district of Petticoat Lane had come to be the undisputed hub of the second-hand trade. Now the Old Clothes Exchange took a key element of the trade off the streets.

It didn't approach the architectural grandeur of, say, the stock or coal exchange. A large plot of damp ground behind an old warehouse was shut off from the street by a hoarding and partly roofed over. Whether selling or buying, it cost a halfpenny to enter the gate. Inside were rows of benches where the hundreds of ol' clo' men and women—not buying now, but selling—would disgorge their sacks and bundles. Every afternoon, between two and four o'clock in winter, an hour or two later in summer, they'd arrive with their day's pickings to find a waiting scrum of buyers—old-clothes dealers and middle-men. Haggling notwithstanding, goods quickly changed hands; here, too, the selling price was typically a quarter of the sum first parlayed.

In the aggregate, a lot of money went through the Old Clothes Exchange each day. But the individual Ol' Clo' man didn't see much of it. Most of what he made of an afternoon went towards buying clothes on the next day's round—or, for the crock-barterer, on buying a new load of china and glass to exchange. Many of them began each week's collecting with cash supplied by moneylenders, which had to be repaid, with interest, on Saturday night.

Mayhew assured visitors to the 1851 Great Exhibition that 'of all the many curious sights in London, there is none so picturesque...none so novel and none so animated as that of the Old Clothes Exchange' at its afternoon peak. It wasn't just the sight of it, but the accumulated stink of all those old clothes, interlaced with the aroma of the hawkers' fare: hot eels, peas and sheep's trotters, hardback (molasses toffee), hot wine, coffee and beer, all for sale within.

In next to no time, the Old Clothes Exchange had become a London institution and for decades nearly all second-hand clothing for sale in the city's markets and shops would have passed through it. Of course, not all—nothing like all—the garments unloaded by the ol' clo' men of an afternoon were fit for resale and wearing. These weren't, for the most part, clothes that people had simply tired of. No, it was the *clothes* that were tired: the best of them would've been faded and frayed, the rest stained, tattered, and worn to holes.*

Before being ready for the retail market, a large proportion of garments from the Old Clothes Exchange would require the attentions of the 'clobberer', the 'reviver' and the 'translator'. Clobberer and reviver were close kin: the former patched and mended, the latter dyed and rejuvenated; both were skilled in deception. 'Of all the wares in this traffic,' Mayhew found, 'the clothing for the feet is what is most easily prepared to cheat the eye.' Few poor people would ever own a new pair of boots or shoes, so there was a terrific demand for second-hand. A clobbering shoemaker would patch worn-through soles with cardboard, cleverly disguised with 'a preparation of dirt,

* And none of them would have been clean. *Clean*, like *new*, was a relative term.

which looks like the dust of the road'. But even shoes with holes were better than none: 'a very poor industrious widow' might, for a few pence, buy her child a pair 'of some sort or other', a shoemaker told Mayhew, adding, 'There's a sort of decency, too, in wearing shoes.' Indeed, many a poor woman went shoeless for the sake of seeing her children shod.

As for the reviver's art, a worn black suit, treated to a dye job, would outfit a lowly clerk or curate who was expected to look respectable on a pittance. Mind you, there'd be no guarantee it was colourfast. A shower of rain and...oh well. The same went for hats. A tall silk hat—what we'd call a top hat—was tall indeed in the nineteenth century, and you could spot a second-hand one by the relative shortness of its crown. The lower portion, where it had sat on the former owner's head, would have been greasy and discoloured with hair oil and sweat. This the reviver cut away, then reaffixed the brim. A merely shabby old hat would be ironed, brushed, glued and dyed to look as good as new. 'But let the wearer beware the first shower...if he would prevent the disclosure of all the deception practised in the renovation of his second-hand hat.' Stained silk dresses and waistcoats were touched up—dry-cleaned, in effect—with turpentine. If a garment was beyond the wiles of the clobberer or reviver, it could be salvaged by the translator, whose skill was in 'translating' one garment into a different one, or even several. An adult's dress or coat might be trimmed of its ragged portions, to leave a scaled-down version suitable for a child. A man's woollen frockcoat, or *surtout*, was considered the most serviceable of all second-hand garments. A sturdy one might go through several owners, passing 'down the scale respectable', before it succumbed to irretrievable seediness. Usually the flared skirts of a coat exhibited the least wear and so would live on as caps and gaiters, or boys' knickerbockers and waistcoats. The salvageable fabric from an expired waistcoat might go to make new 'legs' for a pair of women's cloth boots or, if satin or velvet, would end up as hat linings or yarmulkes.

Most of this repair and remodelling took place in workrooms in the neighbourhood of the Old Clothes Exchange, part of the same busy hive as the street markets where the reworked merchandise was sold. Of course, there were still piles of raw tatt from which a poor woman might buy and do the cutting-down and mending herself. Dresses made of cotton were called 'washing dresses', because, as an Irish ol' clo' woman told Mayhew:

> *Cotton washes, and if a decent woman gets a cheap second-hand cotton, she washes and does it up, and it seems to come to her fresh and new. That can't be done with stuff.*

Second-hand dresses of stuff (that is, wool) or cotton sold for about one shilling and sixpence, less than half the price of silk. And they were snapped up. It was silk dresses that perpetually hung in glossy ranks, 'out of keeping with the rough and dirty-looking aspect of the market itself', and that have survived to populate the costume collections of museums. Workaday dresses were worn, remade and worn again until reduced to rags.

❧

Old clothes mended or transformed before resale were mostly headed for local and domestic markets. But a fair portion of the garments leaving the Old Clothes Exchange were destined, 'as is', for export.* France had been receiving England's cast-offs since at least the sixteenth century. Despite complaints about the dumping of '*vieux chapeaux, bottes et savates*' (old hats, boots and worn-out shoes)—English leather being of superior quality—old boots crossed the Channel by the shipload. Altered to suit French fashions, they sold as better-than-second-hand.

By the 1850s, however, England was exporting second-hand apparel almost everywhere *except* France—whose own export trade in 'old and worn clothing' was booming. Buyers for the export trade packed their purchases from

* Men's garments, anyway; women's and children's were rarely exported.

London's Old Clothes Exchange in bales three metres square, ready for shipping—chiefly to Ireland. In recent decades, Irish merchants quartered around Rosemary Lane had become a significant presence on London's second-hand scene. Some of them bought exclusively for export, shipping clothing bales to Ireland weekly or oftener in a trade that amounted to perhaps a million garments a year.

The plentiful poor of Ireland were objects of pity and scorn to the English. An entry in the *Encyclopaedia Britannica* in 1853 described their 'wretched' clothing—

> *The rags in which both men and women are clothed are so worn and complicated that it is hardly possible to imagine to what article of dress they originally belonged. The dress is worn both night and day, till it literally falls to pieces, and even when first put on it is usually cast-off clothing.*

When buying for Irish export, then, pretty much anything was deemed good enough. 'The old clothes bags of the collectors may, in fact, be said to be emptied out in the land of Erin, as far as the ordinary clothes go,' a writer for *The Times* observed.

And not just ordinary clothes. In an era with no market for 'vintage' gear, garments of antiquated fashion would be consigned to Ireland. There were accounts, well into the twentieth century, of peasants in remoter parts of Ireland dressing in 'tall hat, swallow-tail coat, knee breeches and low boots': essentially the same outfit given to a pantomime Irishman.

It wasn't, as most supposed, Ireland's national costume. It was the echo of fashions cast aside in England more than a hundred years earlier. Likewise, leather breeches had been standard dress for English working men until, in the decades before 1800, cheap sturdy cotton corduroy came along. Two generations later, those old leather breeches would still be doing service in Ireland. And when poor Irishmen did get to wear corduroy, it would take the retrogressive form of knee-breeches, cut down from full-length pantaloons discarded by their English counterparts.

Holland ranked second in demand for England's old clothes. Not just any old clothes, but the decommissioned red coats of the British infantry, which were converted into flannel undergarments. As the exporters understood it, 'There seems to be some popular belief or superstition in that water-logged country that red cloth affords the best protection against rheumatism.'

Others of the iconic red coats, cast-offs from regiments quartered on the Peshawar frontier, became the uniform of Afghanistan's infantry after their rout of the British in 1842. According to a face-saving report in the London press, 'The red coat is held in the highest estimation by the Afghan rulers...a proud instance of the *prestige* the British army acquired in Afghanistan, despite the loss of it.'

The coats of British officers, not merely red but scarlet, went to the great trade fair in Leipzig (famed as Europe's marketplace) and thence to Russia, to make cuffs and trimming for the livery of government officials. Livery was, and is, the name for a non-military uniform worn by functionaries (mayors, magistrates, beadles), members of the royal court or trade guilds, and servants to the high and mighty. Just like military uniform, livery signalled the wearer's rank or their master's identity by means of colour and bling. Appearance, therefore, was everything. Suits would regularly be replaced and reissued, leading to a flourishing market in the second-hand item. At London's Old Clothes Exchange livery and regimentals had their own department, and every day's paper carried advertisements like this one—

> *WANTED, LEFT-OFF CLOTHES, for exportation.—Messrs Levy, of 251, Strand, are giving the highest price, in cash, for LEFT-OFF CLOTHES, Uniforms, Court Dresses, Swords, &c.*

Always, it was 'for exportation' they were wanted. 'I fancy all those sort of things is sent abroad,' an old-clothes seller told Mayhew. 'I don't know where. Perhaps where people doesn't know they was liveries.' Livery, you see, carried a stigma—a double-edged stigma, even: if Lord Hoity didn't want his distinctive livery adorning a costermonger, the coster probably didn't want to be taken for Lord H's 'man', either. As Mayhew's informant put it: 'I wouldn't wear an old livery coat, if it was the Queen's, for five bob.'

There hadn't always been such a taboo. The second Duke of Newcastle had, in his lifetime, sought to prevent the tarnishing of his brand* by rewarding servants to forgo the 'perk' of selling their old liveries. He'd jealously hoarded the cast-offs but, upon his death in 1794, all were sold and 'for a year or two after, scarcely a carter, coachman, or porter in London, but wore the Newcastle livery'.

Still, by mid-century, second-hand liveries were considered 'the great prizes of the profession'. British liveries were in demand in Europe, where their insignia carried no associations. But a good many—along with regimentals and even police uniforms†—were destined for the west coast of Africa, where carpetbaggers and missionaries used them to woo the local 'kings and chiefs'.

* Described as 'eccentric' and 'baroque', his grace was much given to finery and was hailed, in his youth, as the handsomest man in England.

† Established in 1848, the Police Superannuation Fund was supported, in part, by the regular sale of uniforms.

The press at Home made high sport of it, confecting such 'barbaric splendours' as 'a native chief ruling his tribes in the robes of a sheriff of the City of London'.

France, in the same period, exported second-hand in quantities rivalling new clothing to its European neighbours, as well as to North Africa and South America. After the revolution of 1848, Louis-Napoleon reformed the republican-leaning national guard and their old uniforms were shipped to the New World for Haiti's new emperor to outfit *his* militia. The French press, like the British, relished the image of 'Negroes in regimental pomp'. By this time France itself had little use for others' second-hand—except that it would import from England as rags (and so, duty-free) black clothing that was too far gone for reviving. These rags, sent also to Russia and Poland, were used to make the ubiquitous cloth caps worn by working men in those countries.

Throughout the 1850s, adverts appeared daily in the English press seeking 'Left-off clothes for Australia'—including liveries, which, as the droll weekly *Punch* was quick to point out, did 'not say much for the cause of progress in Australia'. Antipodean newspapers and politicians retorted that no such trade existed, the very suggestion being a slight on the go-ahead, gold-rich colonies. *Melbourne Punch* (no relation) wondered, 'What is done with the old clothes continually advertised as wanted for Australia?' and supposed that people back home must imagine 'that this extensive adoption of cast-off clothing [gives] the colonists a very second-hand appearance'.

In fact, what surprised new arrivals to the gold colonies was that men of all classes dressed in the same uniform of new-bought, ready-made clothing: a shirt of red or blue, moleskin trousers and a wide-awake hat. Very often, the clothes that people brought with them from abroad were all wrong or too numerous or both. And some immigrants, it's true, were misled into thinking they'd find a flourishing market for 'clothing of antiquated pattern, shape, and material...unsaleable in the mother country'. London *Punch*'s satiric advice that 'Australia would seem to be in want of a sort of Rag Fair' was, however, redundant. Almost since the Victorian gold rushes began in 1851, newcomers with surplus gear had staged an impromptu bazaar—known, yes, as Rag Fair—on Melbourne's dockside, selling directly from their overflowing trunks. Other gold-seekers lightened their loads by stowing luggage in Melbourne to be sent for later. Many such trunks, left unclaimed at the warehouses, were auctioned, contents and all, to end up back at Rag Fair.

Back home in England, the touted trade in 'Left-off clothing for Australia' would persist well into the 1860s, to the ongoing annoyance of colonists—

> *...the fact is* [spluttered a writer in the *Sydney Morning Herald*] *that not a single article purchased in this manner leaves the old country for these colonies; they are, it is well known, too eagerly sought after and bought up in London, Dublin, &c., to leave any to spare for 'exportation'. But the best of it all is, that they are not wanted here...*

The ruse owed something to the tender feelings of those at Home who hesitated to sell their old clothes for fear that they'd be recognised on the backs of strangers. 'This little fib'—that their cast-offs were wanted 'on the other side of the Pacific'—tended, it was claimed, to dispel such reticence.

To Australians, though, any suggestion that Britain's discards were being dumped here was a freighted reminder of the colonies' beginnings and the lingering stain of convictism. And talk about diehard: in 1883, denying asylum to three Fenian exiles,* the premier of Victoria would assert (amid cheers) that 'Australia won't have, at any price, old England's cast-off clothing or blood-stained criminals'.

* Members of the Irish Republican Brotherhood, whose military arm had assassinated two British government ministers. The exiles had turned informer and been promised asylum.

CHAPTER 3

The Waifs and Strays of Civilisation

'Tis no harm to tell that I pawned, for...a good pledge never shamed its master.

ELLEN WATSON, COUNTY DOWN, IRELAND, 1836

Pawnbroking, as we've seen, grew out of age-old practices of moneylending. In some parts of Europe during the eighteenth century, government-run pawnshops were established as a kind of charitable bank, lending money at low interest to the poor. And not just to the poor. In Paris, the *mont-de-piété* (from the Italian *monte di pieta*—literally 'mount of pity') might give the price of a loaf of bread in exchange for a petticoat, or accept diamonds and silverware from an aristocrat to fund an evening's gambling. The interest paid (if items were redeemed) or the profits from their sale (if not) went towards poor-relief.

Britain bent to no such innovation. There, although subject to regulation, pawnbroking was strictly a private concern. Over the course of the eighteenth century, as populations and consumption grew, pawnbrokers expanded their operations from the cities and ports to industrial towns and inland centres.

In 1836—nearly a decade before the Famine—a British government inquiry considered the effect, for good or ill, of the growing number of pawnshops on 'the Condition of the Poorer Classes' in Ireland. Commissioners heard evidence in every barony and county seat. Downpatrick, a middle-sized town south of Belfast, had three pawnshops where fifteen years earlier there'd been none. Inhabitants of the town could now 'run and pawn something' whenever they were short of food for the table or the price of a glass of whiskey. Even countryfolk living a half-day's walk away would make pilgrimage to the pawnshops for the sake of a shilling or two and, every spring, winter clothes and bedding would be hocked to buy potato and flax seed.

A poor family, if they were lucky, might possess one valuable item solely for use as collateral. The heirloom nightdress trimmed with lace or the fine linen tablecloth would oscillate, weekly or according to the season, between home and pawnshop. Generally though, when money was short, a woman's 'best' dress would be the first to go—that is, if she owned more than one. Otherwise it would be 'the best things we have', starting with undergarments.

Much was made, in evidence to the Irish inquiry, of the pawning by the poor of their meagre possessions—a teapot, shoes, a labourer's tools, 'their day or night-clothes, or whatever they could get anything on'—for the sake of a glass of whiskey. The commissioners, concerned that clothing given as charity might thus be liquidated, were assured that 'so few clothes are given to the poor that they seldom pawn them'. And anyway, those few would be marked by their givers with indelible ink as a deterrent. Concerns were expressed, too, that pawnshops encouraged stealing: by servants from their employers and by 'strolling beggars' from washing lines.

Clothing accounted for between fifty and seventy-five per cent of items pawned. The money loaned, as a percentage of the pledged item's value, seems to have varied a good deal. Alice Kelly of County Monaghan told the commissioners, 'You will get half on anything that is gay and fashionable, and that is sure to sell well, but on an apron or a child's frock, you would not get in the same way'—only, perhaps, a quarter or a third of the item's value. In the cities, where pawnbrokers faced stiff competition, the sum advanced might stretch to three-quarters of a pledge's value, or even higher. But while it may have been true that 'a London pawnbroker will often lend more upon an article than it will sell for', in the provinces advances were 'shamefully mean'—and the poorer the borrower, the meaner the loan.

In the whole of Britain during the year 1869, something like 208 million pledges were lodged, in return for which pawnbrokers advanced more than £40 million. Around the same time, a Melbourne pawnbroker estimated that he had about £1,000 out in loans. Pawnshops were sometimes called 'the poor man's bank' and, like a bank, they were used not just when times were desperate but as a regular part of household business: a means of balancing a budget from week to week and across the year. Still, as one witness told the 1836 inquiry into the Irish poor, 'We think the pawnbrokers a necessary material, but we don't look on it as a decent business.' Unlike the 'charitable banks' on the continent, Britain's pawnshops were for-profit and the cost of banking there wasn't cheap.

Ellen Watson, married to a carter, said of the pawnbrokers in her town: 'This I do know, that they are all three making very good fortunes out of the poor.' She'd been advanced seven shillings and sixpence 'to make up the price of a pig' and, upon redeeming her pledge after less than five months, was charged interest of one-and-tuppence, or 15.5 per cent. The going rate, if a loan ran full-term (usually twelve months), was twenty-five per cent—unless, as wasn't uncommon, the sum lent was less than a shilling, in which case no interest was charged.*

The Irish were relatively new to the business of pawning and it still bore an element of secrecy that, elsewhere, had long worn off. For many Irish, it remained 'a bit of a night job': they would visit the pawnbroker's after dark to avoid being seen by neighbours. For others, necessity as much as habit had quickly diminished any sense of shame. 'At first,' admitted Alice Kelly, 'we used to go in the dusk to the pawnbroker's, but now I would not care if all the people on the Market Cross saw me; they know it is weighty pressure makes us do it.'

A pawnshop customer lodging an item in exchange for a loan received a ticket, which they must produce to redeem the pledge. A pawn ticket—and a household might have several in play at a time—would be kept in a safe place. Otherwise, on a whim, it might be exchanged for a drink and the thing it betokened irretrievably lost. Second-hand tea-caddies fitted with lock and key were in demand among working men's wives, said one of Mayhew's street-sellers, 'as they keep "my uncle's cards" there'.

Pledges of small yet indispensable worth were

* As little as a few pence might be given for an old hat or 'a couple of children's frocks'.

generally redeemed (or 'lifted') by their owners well before the appointed year was up. But if, after twelve months, a borrower was unable to repay the loan, their pledge would be forfeited and sold by the pawnbroker to recoup his outlay. Forfeited items had, by law, to be auctioned ('canted') in the same town where they were lodged, which could make for some awkwardness. The Irish commissioners wanted to know: was it considered taboo to buy a neighbour's coat? And they were answered with contradictions. Bess Hughes of County Monaghan swore that she had never known 'any damp [inhibition] of that kind', adding, 'But still I would not like to wear my neighbour's goods.' In County Armagh, John Cullen was unequivocal: 'Sure, I may as well wear a neighbour's coat as a stranger.' In County Tipperary people 'seldom purchase at the auctions', according to a pawnbroker there, 'but I do not think it arises from any feeling towards their neighbours, or fear of them'. Yet just the opposite was said to be true in County Down, where people, while keen to pick up bargains, would steer clear of clothing—outerwear, anyway—in case it had been a neighbour's.

Besides relying on local bidders, though, provincial auctions might be attended by second-hand merchants from out of town, and goods unsold would find their way to the city for sale. The London export trade to Ireland discussed in chapter 2 would come later, after the Famine.

For now, the Irish market for affordable clothing was fed largely by the 'outleavings' of pawnshops.

Big-city pawnbrokers served Victorian journalists as a reliable source of gaudy pathos, to complement their tableaux of gutter-side squalor. Chronicling seedy 'Night Scenes in Melbourne' for the *Argus* in 1868, the journalist Marcus Clarke itemised what he saw in the storeroom of a busy pawnshop. Here, an abject legion of coats hanging from pegs, 'suggest[s] ideas of suicide'—

> *Here huge boxes are overflowing with shirts; here enormous packing-cases are piled high with boots. Crinolines hang dangling from the rafters, meerschaum pipes are stacked along the walls, concertinas, violins, and cornets-à-piston speak the distress of the musical profession...*

A decade earlier, one of Clarke's journalistic exemplars, George Augustus Sala, had attended a pawnbrokers' auction in London. It was one of the sales of 'Genuine Unredeemed Pledges' staged four times a year by the firm of Debenham and Storr. Characterised by 'much noise, much dust, and an appreciable amount of confusion', such an auction, said Sala, 'is the Bohemianism of commerce'. And didn't he love it.

Sala, like every 'colour' writer of the period, especially appreciated a list. Hinting at a three-volume novel reduced to its constituent parts, an artfully contrived list stoked a reader's imagination like nothing else. No picture could convey as much. Sala's incantation of the auctioneer's lots, long enough to half-fill a broadsheet column, ended with—

> ...two dozen sheepskin coats, warranted from Crimea, a silver-mounted dressing-case, one of eau-de-cologne, an uncut copy of Macaulay's 'History of England', a cornet-à-piston, a buhl inkstand, an eight-day clock, two pairs of silver grape-scissors, a poonah-painted screen, a papier-mâché work-box, an assortment of variegated floss-silk, seven German flutes, an ivory casket, two girandoles for wax candles, an ebony fan, five flat-irons, and an accordion.

True, there were incongruities—those flat-irons—but overall it was an up-market inventory, of a wholly different class from the pledges borrowed against in rural Ireland. Where was the teapot and the palliasse, the labourer's shirt and the apron? In Melbourne, surveying that storeroom full of pledges halfway to unredemption, Clarke reckoned that 'All the odds and ends, the waifs and strays of civilisation, find their way here.' But, of course, he was wrong: not *all*, not by a long shot.

ᔕ

> *The reader must often have perceived in some by-street, in a poor neighbourhood, a small dirty shop, exposing for sale the most extraordinary and confused jumble of old, worn-out, wretched articles...*

This was Dickens, exemplar of exemplars, alluding to the shop of a London 'broker', or marine-stores dealer. Marine-stores dealers were partly the successors of the mediaeval 'upholders' (dealers in second-hand goods generally) and partly their own thing. The maritime-sounding name signified a link with the shipping trade. In the not-too-distant past, they had operated in the ship-chandlery line, supplying rope, sailcloth and the like and—importantly—buying the same things second-hand.* By the Victorian era, though, the marine-stores dealer was a fixture of poor neighbourhoods at whatever distance from the docks.

Akin yet different (if barely so) were the rag-and-bottle shops. Both bought used goods of all and any kinds and condition. The distinction between them was supposed to be that marine-stores dealers bought with a view to reselling as-is, while rag-and-bottle shops re-sold goods as waste or scrap.† By Dickens's time, however, the two were

* In the US, the junk shop got its name by the same route, 'junk' having originally meant old rope.

† For *recycling*, we'd say; only that term had not yet been invented.

close to indistinguishable for our purposes.

By mid-century there were more marine-store shops in the poorest London backstreets than either grocers or beer-sellers. It was to them, not to a pawnbroker, that a person might take their teapot if they needed thruppence. And for a penny more, they might buy it back in a few days if it hadn't been sold. Teapots were among the items that big-city pawnbrokers, at that date, declined to accept as pledges. Other kitchen implements would likewise be refused, as would anything else classed as 'lumber': bedding, mended boots or trousers (or those in need of mending), and 'common pictures'. Given that they would buy anything, the marine-stores dealer was regarded as more or less synonymous with a receiver of stolen goods—colloquially, a 'fence'. A 1797 pamphlet listing 'Persons who are Supposed to Support Themselves In and Near the Metropolis by Pursuits Either Criminal, Illegal, Or Immoral', included: 'Receivers of Stolen Goods, from petty Pilferers, at Old Iron Shops, Store Shops, Rag and Thrumb* Shops, and Shops for Second-hand Apparel'. The author put the number of such receivers in London at around four thousand. In Field Lane, where Dickens situated Fagin's den, shops of the marine-stores sort 'display[ed] their goods, as sign-boards to the petty thief'.

* Thrumb = rope.

The marine-stores dealer, besides paying money for anything, might also accept, on pledge, items which their owner was 'unwilling to part finally with'. Not all such shops offered pawnbrokerage to the poor, but those that did advertised the fact by hanging above their door 'a black doll in a white frock, with two faces—one looking up the street, the other looking down'. Hence, although the sign-board may have read 'Dealer in Marine Stores', they were known as 'dolly shops'. Unlike pawnbrokers, dolly shops were unregulated and, if the service they provided was an essential one to the poor, it was also mighty lucrative to the dolly-man. For a loan of tuppence advanced on a saucepan, interest of ha'penny a week was charged—and it was due even if the loan were repaid next day. Mayhew did the arithmetic. 'A halfpenny a day interest on a loan of 2d is at the rate of 7280 per cent *per annum*!' and called the system 'positively monstrous'.

Many of the street-hawkers of 'old metal articles' or 'miscellaneous commodities' whom Mayhew encountered were in the employ of marine-stores dealers. Usually it was a barrow business, due to the cumbrousness of their inventory. Other times, a marine-stores man who found himself with an excess of stock might set up pitches, or stalls, along the street, in the charge of his wife and children.

Mayhew summarised the barrow-man's stock as 'an

extensive variety of broken or faded things', noting that demand had dropped for second-hand boxing gloves, fans and back-boards 'to make girls grow straight'. But, when it came to the seller of old metal, he gave in to the enumerating urge. As well as knives and forks and the commonplace tools of the carpenter, he listed (in part)—

> *...old scissors and shears; locks, keys, and hinges; shovels, fire-irons, trivets, chimney-cranes, fenders, and fire-guards; warming-pans...flat and Italian irons, curling-tongs; rings, horse-shoes and nails; coffee and tea-pots, urns, trays, and canisters, pewter measures; scales and weights; bed-screws and keys; candlesticks and snuffers...tobacco and snuff-boxes and spittoons; door-plates, numbers, knockers, and escutcheons; dog-collars and dog-chains (and other chains); gridirons; razors; coffee-mills; lamps; swords and daggers; gun and pistol-barrels and locks (and occasionally the entire weapon); bronze and cast metal figures; table, chair, and sofa castors; bell-pulls and bells...compositors' sticks; the multifarious kinds of tin-wares; stamps; cork-screws; barrel-taps; ink-stands; a multiplicity of culinary vessels and of old metal lids...broken machinery, and parts of machinery,* [such] *as odd wheels, and screws of all sizes, &c., &c.*

One canny old-metal man confided that he kept his metal goods 'all rough and rusty' because customers, when they saw an item ready-cleaned and shiny, suspected trickery. Besides, 'Folks like to clean up a thing themselves, and it's as if it was something made from their own cleverness.' More second-hand pistols were for sale on the streets after 1851 than before, another barrow-man told Mayhew, because 'people were afraid the foreigners coming to the Great Exhibition had some mischief in their noddles, and so a pistol was wanted for protection'. A seller who specialised in metal trays presented a somewhat circular argument as to their quality: 'if they hadn't been real good trays at first, they would never have lived to be second-hand ones'. (That's as neat a distillation of the second-hand ethos as you're likely to come across.)

So, marine-stores dealers sold, either at their shop or in the streets, any goods fit for re-use in their existing form. The bulk of their business, though, was as a conduit for waste products suitable for recycling—which, as the next chapter will show, comprised anything from building materials to kitchen scraps, besides things undreamt of by us.

In Dickens's archetypal 'small dirty shop', there were corners dedicated to 'old iron and bones, and heaps of mildewy fragments of woollen-stuff and linen'. In a 'respectable' marine-stores shop visited by Mayhew, a mass of old iron awaited the foundry furnace, while the entire shop floor was 'intricate' with goods awaiting sorting and selling-on: wastepaper, bottles,* bones, broken furniture, unclobberable boots, clothing and linen fit only for rags. In less congested locales, a marine-stores dealer's stock would spill out into a yard.

A good proportion of this stuff came to the marine-stores shop through street-buyers or collectors, broadly known as rag-and-bone or rag-and-bottle men. Like the ol' clo' men, they walked the streets, dealing with householders and servants at kitchen doors, either on behalf of a marine-stores dealer or on their own account. But customers also sold their refuse direct to the shops—not just the marine-stores shops but, you'll remember, the rag-and-bottle shops whose specialty this was.

The fronts of such shops might be painted a bright colour for easy recognition even by the illiterate. Handbills or street-criers would put out the word that the 'red house' or the 'blue house' gave the best price for waste-stuff. Mayhew quoted from the handbill of a London Rag, Bottle & Kitchen Stuff Warehouse that sought 'Furniture and Lumber of every description', bones, and bottles of all kinds ('Eau de Cologne, Soda Water, Doctor's Bottles, Phials & Broken Flint Glass'), as well as—

* Empty bottles got the name 'marines', or 'dead marines', from the marine-stores shop.

Old Copper, Brass, Pewter, &c.
Lead, Iron, Zinc, Steel, &c., &c.
Old Horse Hair, Mattresses, &c.
Old Books, Waste Paper, &c.
White Linen Rags
All Kinds of Coloured Rags.

Rag-and-bottle shops, marine-stores dealers—whatever they called themselves, they were everywhere in an age when necessity, more than virtue, dictated that there was 'no such thing as waste'.

CHAPTER 4

No Such Thing as Waste 1: The Humble Rag

In nature there is no such thing as waste; nothing, in fact, is lost...

DR ANDREW WYNTER, IN *CASSELL'S FAMILY PAPER*, 1865

I wrote a few chapters back that a rag isn't a rag while it can still be worn. Even once consigned to ragdom, it might not stay a rag for long. This is less true now than it was, but still, a rag is a mutable thing.

Rags must have been used for cleaning and polishing ever since humans first had that inclination. Until just a few years ago a neighbour of mine, a woman in her nineties, would spread out her dusters—old singlets worn to holes—on a lavender bush to dry. A household, in times past, would have kept a supply of clean rags for medicinal use, as bandages, dressings and poultices. Rags made workaday apron-fronts and kerchiefs (do-rags), as well as sanitary napkins, hair-curlers, nappies and bibs. And stuffing: pillows, bolsters, footstools, draught-excluders. In the British Museum there's a Roman doll stuffed with rags, perhaps 1,800 years old.

So there was value in rags as a household commodity. But rags—the right sort of rags, the commonest rags—were worth money too, not so much *as rags* as for their suggestible composition. As the industrial age gained full steam, it was rags that were most sought after by marine-stores men and their legions of collectors. Rags were traded across borders and oceans or—a sure mark of value—were in some countries *outlawed* from export. And the industries driving the market for the humble rag were three: paper, shoddy and flock.

Rags as a market commodity were unknown before the sixteenth century, when paper displaced parchment and vellum in the uncloistered age of print. At first, the rags used by paper-makers were of linen (fabric made from the flax plant) because there was as yet no real cotton industry. That would change over the course of two hundred years, with slave-worked plantations blooming in the New World, the invention of the spinning jenny and the harnessing of steam. By the nineteenth century, cotton rags far outnumbered those of linen.

While linen would remain in demand for best-quality paper, coarse brown paper was made from old hemp rope and canvas. Brown-paper mills were set up close to ports and, in London, scavengers known as mudlarks—mostly young boys—combed the docks and shoreline for scraps of rope. Some of them took a pre-emptive approach, cutting the ropes off ships in dock. Marine-stores shops—the middle-men—paid a ha'penny a pound for rope sold wet and half as much again for dry.

But it was cotton rags that fed the mills turning out paper for the newspaper, publishing and stationery trades, all of which swelled in step with literacy and educational reform, with mobility and the spread of empire, and with the expansion of the middle class. Always, one thing fed another. Here old clothes ended up propagating Darwin's theory of evolution, mapping new territory, notating tunes for a parlour piano, blueprinting railway bridges and steamships.

In gold-rush Melbourne (Rag Fair notwithstanding) unwanted clothing was strewn about 'on every unoccupied piece of land'. Opposite the gaol, at the north end of town, tons of discarded clothes lay rotting. It was only when the gold-fever began to cool that the rags gained value and were gathered up for pulping into paper. Soon railways led to Melbourne from all parts of inland Victoria and the cargo of rags to the paper-mills was unflagging.

On the American frontier, newspaper production, that key booster of progress, was occasionally hampered by a shortage of rags. Hence, from Utah in 1861, came a report that due to such a shortage 'The *Deseret News* failed to appear last week.' The implication—that if the district's inhabitants weren't parting with their rags, they must be wearing them—posed a further blight to Deseret's prospects. In the event, Fort Crittenden, a military outpost just then being disbanded, had rags to spare.

In fact, there was a shortage of rags not just in Deseret, Utah, but in America generally for much of the nineteenth century. The nation's paper mills were the destination for most of Britain's rag exports, together with rags from Germany, Austria, Italy and Turkey. For nearly four decades spanning the mid-century, America's rag imports increased by around twenty-five per cent *every year*.

Britain also imported rags from Europe—about ten thousand tonnes per annum, mid-century. These were rags of linen for use in high-quality paper, originating in countries where the wearing of cotton was almost unknown. By this time Britain had, conversely, so far perfected the making and selling of cheap cotton that linen rags were increasingly rare. What little linen there was tended to be hoarded for home-doctoring. So valuable was linen and so increasingly hard to come by that American rag dealers imported Egyptian mummies (exhumed *en masse* during a hundred-year looting spree by antiquarians) for their linen wrappings.*

Linen was preferred by paper-makers not just for its composition but for its colour—or rather, lack of it. White rags were valued over others for the smooth, unspotted quality of the paper they produced. London rag-buyers, calling door to door, might pay a ha'penny a pound for coloured rags, rising to tuppence for clean white. Of domestic (as opposed to imported) rags, those from Scotland were the best regarded and those from Ireland the worst. Dirty and coloured rags were consigned to the cheapest grades of paper, except for blue rags which made the distinctive blue writing paper of the civil service, as well as tobacco papers. At the paper mill, rags were sorted and torn into small pieces before being mixed in vats with a lime solution that reduced them to a fibrous pulp. Chlorine bleach was introduced to the mix around mid-century, after which rag-dealers became colour-blind, or nearly so: white linen was still the *ne plus ultra*.

A perpetual want of rags in the US spurred the paper industry's search for alternatives. Cotton shortages during the Civil War sharpened the necessity, and paper made

* Just as incredible, mummified cats were dug up and imported by the thousand, because their bituminous coating made them ideal fuel for steam engines.

from wood pulp was first produced in that decade. By the early 1880s, most US newspapers were printed on wood-based stock and, in the coming decades, the rest of the world followed.

For much of the nineteenth century Britain was, as Marx wrote, 'the emporium for the rag trade of the whole world'. It continued to be, even as the US paper trade grew more self-sufficient. On top of its domestic rag harvest, Britain's annual imports topped thirty thousand tonnes in the mid-1870s. These weren't all linen rags, or even cotton; woollen rags, too, were in demand—for the shoddy mills.

Shoddy, before it meant 'poor quality' or 'sham', was the name of a fabric woven (or re-woven) from waste wool—either rags, or factory and tailors' clippings. The adjectival shoddy was, you might say, a by-product. From the invention of the process, early in the century, the shoddy industry grew fast, centring around the northern town of Leeds. And over the decades, the process would be refined so that even the most refractory of textiles could be absorbed into new.

At the shoddy mills, enormous toothed wheels ground the woollen rags into fibres, which were then 'worked up' with a small quantity of fresh wool to make new cloth. It was reckoned, in the mid-1860s, that the wool content of rags fed into Yorkshire's shoddy mills annually was equal to the fleece of eight million sheep. The rags arrived at the mill in bales, which were opened in a vast sorting room and their contents 'piled in close, poverty-smelling masses upon the floor'. Rag-workers, almost exclusively girls and women, sorted the rags by colour and coarseness, ripping out linings, cutting off hooks and buttons, and emptying pockets so that nothing but wool went into the mill. In *Das Kapital*, Marx singled out rag-sorting as 'one of the most shameful, the most dirty, and the worst paid kinds of labour'.

The wheels that ground the rags were called 'devils', and their action sent up 'choking clouds of dry pungent dirt and floating fibres' known as 'devil's dust'. Mill workers would be 'powdered to a dull greyish hue' and of course they inhaled the dust, resulting in 'shoddy fever', a debilitating lung complaint. There being, after all, 'no such thing as waste', devil's dust was itself harvested to create the plush textured wallpapers that looked so well by gaslight.

By mid-century, the use of shoddy had made new clothing affordable for many who'd never worn other than second-hand. The men's coat trade particularly profited from shoddy, creating such fast-fashion lines as piumas, pardessus, siphonias, ponchos, talmas, trevalions, caracos, himalayas, salamancas, petershams and chesterfields. Countless styles of coat, exhibiting little variation except in name, were retailed and extensively advertised by drapers who were perfectly happy to be branded as 'cheap clothing establishments'. Indeed it was shoddy that marginalised second-hand clothing, making it the resort of the poorest. Shoddy was cheap; but was it any good?

W. B. Ferrand, a British MP, led a campaign in the 1840s that portrayed shoddy as degenerate and un-British. To demonstrate the flimsiness of the fabric, 'a preparation of wool made from thrice-worn and greasy old clothes of Europe', Ferrand tore a piece to shreds in Parliament. The fibre produced by the devil was short and brittle—more pulp, really, than fibre—and even with a quantity of fresh wool added, the resultant fabric was unstable. Uniforms made by US shoddy mills during the Civil War were of such poor quality that, in a shower of rain, they would 'melt' back into pulp; in fact *shoddy* became a byword for wartime profiteers.

Australia was well supplied with shoddy apparel from England, much to the chagrin of colonial woolgrowers. Their wool 'is now returned to us, after paying two freights and several commissions, largely mixed with a pulp called shoddy'. To pass shoddy off as wool was fraudulent, declared the protectionist press, and 'the people who purchase it would be better off in the long run if they gave a preference to colonial tweed over imported shoddy'.

Second-hand clothes sellers made a similar argument. As the market for shoddy had grown, they'd seen their industry shrink. A frockcoat or its fancy-named equivalent could be bought for a guinea (twenty-one shillings) at the cheap clothing establishments—in fact, the 'guinea coat' was their signature product line. That was cheap all right, if nowhere near as cheap as second-hand. But that wasn't the argument. As one old-clothes dealer told Mayhew:

> *...if you find a slop* thing marked a guinea, I don't care what it is, but I'll undertake that you shall get one that'll wear longer, and look better to the very last, second-hand, at less than half the money, plenty less. It was good stuff and good made at first, and hasn't been abused, and that's the reason why it always bangs a slop—because it was good to begin with.*

Given the ephemeral nature of shoddy, the same man worried doubly for the future of his trade: 'where's the second-hand things to come from?'

Twenty-five years later, the old-clothes business had fallen 'very low indeed' and a man who'd followed the trade all that time blamed the slump on 'the pride of the working classes...and fashion, sir, fashion!'

* Slop = cheap ready-made.

> *Fashions used to last a lifetime, and coats were worn till their owners tired of them, and they went down the scale respectable to dress the labouring classes. But labourers now ape their masters, and buy at first-hand, because they would be gentlemen on their many holidays…We live in a flashy age—nothing solid, nothing substantial—all show and tinsel!*

That very state of things elsewhere formed the basis for a pallid defence of shoddy as the democratic cloth. 'The cloth is not really bad,' wrote one journalist—

> *…it is only a little weaker than whole-wool material. It will not wear so long, nor withstand so much friction; but then it is not always required that clothes shall wear long—rather that they shall look pretty for a time.*

Here was aspirational capitalism in action. Pride, status and fashion dictated that, if a person could afford to buy new, they would. Quality be damned: there'd be no second-hand for them.

But hold on: that guinea coat…did it really qualify as *new*? After all, wasn't shoddy made from reconstituted cast-offs—and not just cast-offs, but those too far gone to be revived? 'No man can say that the materials of the coat he is wearing have not already been on the back of some greasy beggar.' G. A. Sala cast shoddy in evolutionary terms, as 'a perpetual round of mutation and transmutation going on among clothes'. And the transmutation didn't end there.

Old clothes rejected by the rag-sorters as too ruined even for shoddy were designated 'land rags' and sent as fertiliser to the hop-growing districts. Hops, reputedly a 'difficult' plant, loved no manure better than land rags. And never did manure lend itself to such transmigrational musings: 'Thus, the final destination of old clothes after all is the human frame, [but] instead of clothing this vile corpus, they are transmuted into the body itself as we quaff the foaming tankard.'

Even more arcane uses were found for degraded woollen rags. 'Melted' over heat with shavings of hoofs and horns, horse blood, wood ashes and bits of scrap iron, they produced a cyanic substance that went to make exquisite Prussian blue dye. (How does that not qualify as alchemy?) That dye, in turn, gave colour to cloth from which new clothing was made—and so the perpetual round continued.

Transmutation hit a bump, however, in the form of 'union fabrics' in which cotton was interwoven with the wool. Such fabrics as muslin-delaines or winseys* were popular, being lighter in weight and cheaper than whole

* Winsey = a back-to-front contraction of *linsey-woolsey* (literally linen + wool, but used by Shakespeare it meant 'gibberish').

wool. But what use were they, once spent? A 'pretty' process on show at the London International Exhibition of 1862 employed high-pressure steam to separate the constituent elements of mixed-fibre rags. The wool was reduced to a crumbly brown substance, high in nitrogen, that made a fine manure for broccoli, leaving behind the cotton fibre for use at the paper mills.

More intransigent still was silk. True, a small amount derived from old bandana handkerchiefs had been incorporated into the paper of early banknotes to discourage counterfeiting. But by and large, silk was the only fibre to defy the transmutational wizardry of the high industrial age. Mayhew found it paradoxical: 'Though one of the most beautiful and costly of textile fabrics, its "remains" are thrown aside, when a beggar's rags are preserved and made profitable.' Thrown aside perhaps, but some of the exotic rejects have survived in captivity—enough to skew modern perceptions of nineteenth-century dress.

Another name given to the fibrous devil's dust that choked shoddy workers and texturised the papered walls of boudoirs was *flock*. The word had a sheepish origin, meaning a lock of wool, and was applied, in the first place, to waste wool in its raw state used for filling pillows and mattresses. But by the end of the nineteenth century, it wasn't shoddy or paper that consumed the most rags, but the manufacture of flock. Flock no longer meant wool;

rags of any fabric would do. That the word was often prefixed with *common* hints at how things stood with flock. 'Uncleansed', 'unsavoury', 'possibly loathsome' rags of who-knew-what origin were chewed up at the flock mills and spat out as stuffing for mattresses and upholstery. An article titled 'Filth' in a Melbourne newspaper drew attention to the blight cast over certain suburbs by the flock mills that congregated there. It wasn't just the stink of all those old rags or the dust generated by the devils, but the fear of rag-borne infectious diseases.

Early in the twentieth century, the sanitation movement would address the problem of flock. In Glasgow, it was reported, an intrepid sanitary inspector examined the contents of 2,471 mattresses stuffed with 'common flock' and found that 'No attempt at cleansing or disinfecting had been made, and the condition of the material was filthy in the extreme.' Findings like these led to laws requiring that rags be washed and fumigated before being fed to the flock mills.

In the sorting room, rag-workers would set aside any good-quality wool textiles for selling to the shoddy mills. They also kept a sharp eye out for silk stockings, which the friction of the devil's teeth could set alight. The Fletcher family ran a flock mill in Launceston, Tasmania, for fifty-odd years. Not long before World War II, the mill was still going strong, buying up rags and turning out 'clean, wholesome flock'. About one-fifth of every tonne of rags put through the mill was left behind as flock dust—'a mixture of dirt and fluff'—which ended up on Fletchers' farm, as fertiliser.

Every city had mills like Fletchers' advertising daily in the press and sending collectors house-to-house in search of 'cast-off clothes and rags, any quantity'. And every well-managed household kept a rag bag, but not necessarily for sale. Buyers for the flock mills had to compete with the craze for homemade quilts and rugs—

> *You mothers of girls, do you not find your attics and closets continually filling up with cast-off clothing that…seems fit for nothing but the rag bag, and yet too good to be consigned to that end? Here is a use for just such things. Make them into rag rugs.*

Half a kilogram of rags, torn into strips, roughly translated into a woven rug one metre square. A writer in the women's pages of a Melbourne newspaper boasted of making 'a most artistic rug' using an assortment of her children's worn-out socks, the scorched blanket off the ironing board, and an old polka-dot dress.

Hard-up families had long relied on their own version of 'common flock' for making rugs and mattresses. A cover of calico, pieced together from flour or sugar bags, would be filled with scraps of blankets, old clothes, socks—anything woollen—and roughly quilted together in a kind of 'rag sandwich'. (The wagga rug, a vital component of any swagman's kit, was similarly constructed of layered hessian bags,* sewn together with twine.)

In the 1920s came the Economical Rug Machine, touted as the 'greatest invention for the home' and capable of producing a rug from cast-off clothing in just one hour. That was a far cry from the onerous 'few hours a day for a fortnight' needed to make a woolly rug out of old cardigans and college blazers, as demonstrated in classes run by the Housewives' Association in Adelaide during the Depression. Depending on the artistry employed, the making of a decorative patchwork quilt from clothing scraps might be even more time-consuming. Purpose-made heirlooms, some of these old quilts live on as relics of women's work, ancestral wardrobes and the good that may come of cheating the devil.

* Such bags commonly bore the brand of the Murrumbidgee Milling Company of Wagga Wagga, which gave the utilitarian wagga its name.

CHAPTER 5

No Such Thing as Waste 2: the Insatiate Bag of the Waste Collector

The principle which guides him is that everything is useful to someone somewhere.

SAID OF MONSIEUR VERDIER-DUFOUR, MASTER RAG-PICKER, PARIS, 1907

Rags went to make paper, and old paper went to make new paper. Well, eventually it did.

Back when Henry VIII dissolved the monasteries, before paper was a thing, parchment from looted books and documents was put to use as window coverings in Yorkshire cottages, and for patching sails and tarpaulins. Four hundred years later, a 1930s fad for faux-Elizabethan architecture and décor (dubbed 'stockbrokers' Tudor') would see thousands of antique title deeds cut up to make parchment lampshades. Fashion dictated that each shade feature a decorative 'illuminated' capital letter, of which there was only one to a deed, so 'The attrition,' as antiquarian Ivor Noël Hume wrote, 'was not unlike the slaughtering of elephants to take only their tusks.'

Paper mills had begun trying wastepaper as an alternative to rags in the 1850s. But old paper, before that and for a good while after, was used mainly for kindling fires, as wrapping-stuff, or cut into squares for the outhouse. Like rags, it was worth money—a penny or two a pound. Street-buyers went door to door and it piled up at the marine-stores dealer's before he sold it on. A dealer might be called to 'clear out' a lawyer's office, carrying away old briefs and legal papers by the hundredweight. Tax- and rate-collectors, publishers, printers, public houses and coffee shops—all had old paper to unload. What kinds of paper? Here's an (abridged) list put together by Mayhew—

> *...modern poems or pamphlets and old romances (perfect or imperfect), Shakespeare, Moliere, Bibles, music, histories, stories, magazines, tracts to convert the heathen...auctioneers' catalogues and long-kept letters, children's copybooks and last century ledgers, printed effusions which have progressed no further than the unfolded sheets, uncut works and books mouldy from age...*

'I can't read very much,' a wastepaper dealer told him, 'and don't understand about books. I take the backs off and weighs them…and there's an end.' He let Mayhew fossick through some paper, a couple of pennies' worth, bound for a butcher's shop.

> *I found three perfect numbers of a sixpenny periodical, published a few years back. Three, or rather two and a half, numbers of a shilling periodical, with 'coloured engravings of the fashions'. Two (imperfect) volumes of French Plays, an excellent edition…A music sheet, headed, 'A lonely thing I would not be'.*

Wastepaper was in demand not only by butchers, but also bakers, butter sellers, fishmongers, poulterers, confectioners, tobacconists and chandlers (small grocers). And cheesemongers. Regretting that so many of the unwanted pamphlets he handled were of a religious character, Mayhew's informant added, 'I've heard of a page around a quarter of cheese, though, touching a man's heart.' (And what had it touched, I wonder, before it touched the cheese?) Most folks seem to have thought nothing of bringing home sausages wrapped in newsprint or sherbet lemons twisted in a page from Ecclesiastes.

As demand grew at the US paper mills for wastepaper to recycle, historical documents were sacrificed to the cause. In Philadelphia, forty tons of papers from the Bank of America, including letters written by the nation's founders, were sold for pulping in 1857. Even more went to the mills during the cotton shortage that came with the Civil War. An enterprising wastepaper dealer in Washington found a way to capitalise on the 'folly of printing public documents'. Every member of Congress was entitled to twenty copies of any government report. When, in 1872, the report of the joint committee on 'southern outrages' (known as the Ku Klux Conspiracy Report)* was published, it filled thirteen substantial volumes. The wastepaper dealer, figuring that no Democrat would care to peruse that report,† approached every Democratic member of Congress and obtained a signed order for their twenty sets—that is, 260 volumes for each member. Presented at the printing office, these orders entitled him to take possession of thousands of volumes, which he then sold to a paper mill at 3½ cents a pound, amassing a small fortune.

Before the end of the nineteenth century, with affluence and literacy on the rise, most urban households took at least one daily newspaper and perhaps a weekly magazine or two. Once read, all that paper mounted up, until what had been a precious commodity started to become

* Its proper title was *Report of the Joint Select Committee to Inquire into the Condition of Affairs in the Late Insurrectionary States.*

† Remember, Abraham Lincoln was a Republican. Well into the twentieth century, it would be the Democratic Party in the southern states that enforced segregation, resisted civil rights and supplied the ranks of the KKK.

a nuisance. As was the case with rags, women were encouraged to find creative uses for wastepaper: not just to line drawers and shelves or insulate chicken coops, but in decorous pastimes like decoupage and scrapbooking.

And, of course, households would continue to need wastepaper for lighting fires and stoves, and even, in the absence of other fuel, to keep them burning. Ivor Noël Hume, living in London during the straitened years that followed World War II discovered his landlady stoking the basement furnace with books from a trunk left behind by a Polish officer. Hume managed to save just one volume, a rare legal text published in 1510—minus its vellum covers, which had already gone up in smoke.

The kitchen stove that relied on waste for its kindling in turn produced waste that could be sold and put to new uses. That a market existed for second-hand food is surprising enough, but Mayhew took the view that some food qualified as second-hand even the *first* time it came to table. He meant offal, ostensibly a waste product of the slaughtering process—though, of course, nothing that 'comes out of a bullock' *was* wasted.* But even leaving offal aside as questionably second-hand, there was a whole world of 'kitchen-stuff'—scraps and slops and leftovers—that still had its uses.

* Even the leg bones went to make toothbrush handles or dominoes.

Plate-scrapings, pot-scourings, vegetable peelings, dishwater and food gone bad went collectively by the name hogs-wash, being only 'fit for pigs'. In the busy kitchens of hotels, coffee houses, clubhouses, workhouses and prisons, the slops would be thrown in tubs emptied daily by the hogs-wash man, who paid for the privilege. Not all table scraps went into the tub, however. Buckingham Palace leftovers were issued, by a ticket system, to the deserving poor. And 'broken meat' and leavings from respectable institutions like Lincoln's Inn were bought by corner grocers and re-sold as cheap food to the poor. Leftover scraps of pie crust with perhaps a mite of the filling attached were street-food, sold in cones of old paper at a penny or two a helping. 'Among the best customers for this second-hand food,' observed Mayhew, 'were women of the town of the poorer class, who were always ready, whenever they had a few pence at their command, to buy what was tasty, cheap, and ready-cooked.' Fast food, in other words.

Dripping, and kitchen fat generally, was worth money. Usually, in a servant-run household, dripping went as a perk to the cook or charwoman, who sold it to a marine-stores shop, who sold it in turn to a tallow-works for making candles or soap. In even the best-supervised of kitchens, an innocuous pot of dripping might provide the means by which the odd pilfered silver spoon would be smuggled out the back door—a perk within a perk.

Bones also went to the marine-stores shop or with the rag-and-bone man who cried his trade in the streets. Some eventually would find their way back to the kitchen in the form of gelatine or knife handles. Otherwise, bones might be used to make buttons, fertiliser, glue or the charcoal used in sugar refining. For decades after the extermination of the American bison, a lucrative industry was made of their bones, gathered on the Great Plains and sent east by railroad.

Back in the kitchen, bread scraps might also be kept separate from hogs-wash, for feeding to chickens or beggars. But there was a trade, too, in old bread. Roasting and sieving produced breadcrumbs, as well as a fine burnt residue used to make tooth-cleaning powder and the 'chicory' that sold as a cheap alternative to coffee.

And then there were tea leaves. Used tea leaves, like most things used, were sold at kitchen doors and marine-stores shops, the usual sellers being housemaids and charwomen, who were entitled to the tea leaves—not for selling, but to scatter on carpets, settling the dust as they swept. A widow who bought tea leaves, by arrangement, at numerous houses in her neighbourhood told Mayhew, 'I don't know what they're wanted for, but I've heard they're mixed with new tea.' She was being disingenuous for a good reason: it was illegal to manufacture 'new' tea using old leaves, though their sale and collection wasn't explicitly outlawed. Her second-hand leaves would be sold on, dried and dyed, then mixed with a quantity of fresh tea and passed off at the grocers as new.

This spurious tea was foisted on 'the adult tea-drinking poor', a demographic that (neatly) included the chief tea-leaf traffickers—charwomen being renowned as prodigious drinkers of tea.* And indeed, Mayhew reported a complaint widespread among his informants that the strength of tea was so diminished by its half-and-half composition that to make a satisfying cuppa required twice the tea it used to. It stood to reason that, as the dregs from spurious tea went into the manufacture of still spuriouser tea, *ad infinitum*, the pick-me-up would eventually be reduced to dishwater.

ᔕ

Just as everyday clothing is under-represented in museum collections, so little survives in the way of common household furniture from centuries prior to the twentieth. Silk dresses are posed alongside quality antiques, while the utilitarian pieces that furnished kitchen and washhouse—now aggrandised as 'vernacular'—are scarcely

* Charwomen and tea seemed linked even by etymology; but while *char* (like *chore*, meaning an odd job) comes from Old English, *char* as a slang term for tea is Chinese in origin.

to be found. Once it was past all other use, old wooden furniture made fuel for the fire. Likewise, a timber house pulled down or left derelict would be fair game for scavengers seeking reusable materials or firewood. The Globe Theatre, in Shakespeare's time, was built partly with materials brought across the river from a theatre demolished in Shoreditch. And if timber lent itself to reiteration, so did stone. After the monasteries were dissolved in the sixteenth century and their contents had been sold and looted, they were soon picked clean by 'poor people' of anything portable in the way of architectural features: 'by night and by day...they do resort as long as any door, window, iron, glass, or loose lead remains'. Then only the crumbling hulks of the monasteries were left, to serve for generations as 'the great national quarry', a ready source of building stone, masonry and lime.

Wood, stone, leftovers...was there *anything* that qualified as waste? Where the direst poverty existed, the answer was no. There was a market for cigar ends picked up in the streets and for dog turds, ditto (sold to tanneries). And *dustman* wasn't just an old name for garbage collector: a dustman actually dealt in household dust. Mainly, it was the ash from stoves and fireplaces, along with floor- and yard-sweepings. Collected by the dustman, it was carted to a dust-yard and dumped in a great heap from which a swarm of workers—women and children, mostly—would extract bucket- and barrowloads for sifting and sorting. The finest siftings would be sold for making bricks or as manure for clover pasturage. Cinders went as fuel to the brick-kilns. Bits of old brick, gravel and oyster shells were used by builders and road-makers in laying foundations. And from among the dust, the sharp-eyed sorters would pick out odd nubbles of metal, bone and leather—all saleable commodities—and even coins and jewellery, which they might, if careful, pocket as perks of an otherwise unrewarding occupation.

Children in poor families might be sent out to scavenge in the streets or along the shoreline. Scraps of coal or food they would take home; anything else they'd sell. Some street-buyers of rags, bones, bottles, old metal, whatever, would entice child scavengers with the promise of paper windmills or a puppet show. And never was there a surer incentive to the recycling impulse than the arrival of a travelling circus.

> *The children of a city or town seem to know if it's coming by a kind of intuition, and prepare accordingly...scrap metal, old paper, &c., do substantial service in the way of securing the amount of an admission fee.*

Intuition *and* advertisement. Barnum and Bailey's newspaper splash (the source of the advisory above) doubtless triggered a frenzy of rag-and-bottle scavenging among children in Queensland ahead of an 1888 visit by 'The Greatest Show on Earth'. The lead-up to Guy Fawkes night would likewise see every street and yard picked clean of bottles; but then a ha'penny—exchangeable for two fistfuls of lollies—was welcome anytime. With good reason were bottle- and scrap-merchants accused of promoting juvenile crime by offering ready cash, no questions asked, to their legions of young suppliers.

Collecting, sorting and scavenging not only kept valuable raw materials in steady circulation, but spared civic authorities from dealing with refuse. Garbage collection, as a public service, was instituted in Paris at a relatively early date, as part of the same regulating impulse that uncoiled large portions of the city into boulevards you could shoot a cannon down. Each night, Parisians would empty their garbage onto the street outside their houses, allowing *chiffoniers* (literally, rag-pickers) the night hours to rummage through it before the licensed collectors came with their carts at daybreak. Like their London counterparts, *chiffoniers* gathered not just rags but anything reusable or recyclable. Each carried a hook or spiked stick, a bag and a lantern. They usually worked in small family groups: a barrow or sack would be left at a central point; they would fan out from there and return throughout the night to deposit their hoard.

In 1883, with public health a growing concern, Paris's prefect, Eugène Poubelle, decreed that each household's garbage must be placed in a lidded box* on the street, with *chiffoniers* permitted just one hour to go through the bins before the dust cart was due. A new pecking order among *chiffoniers* was quickly established. The first rank, called *placiers*, paid for the right to enter buildings and yards and search the bins before they were put out on the kerb. *Coureurs*, the rag-pickers left on the street, then had to make do with second-hand trash and just the hour before dawn to pick through it.

Presumably that 'hour before dawn' might stretch out to two or three, since the dust cart only began its rounds at first light. At any rate, rag-pickers had to be off the streets by eleven in the morning. Once home, they examined and sorted their harvest and in the mid-afternoon they took the saleable portion to one of the *maître chiffoniers*, or master rag-pickers. There, girls and women were employed as expert sorters, able to distinguish by glance or touch more than forty classes of rag, twenty-six of paper, fifteen of broken glass, and so on. 'It needs almost the subtle eye of a Turner,' wrote an observer, 'to do the work with the necessary accuracy and speed.' They knew which kinds of bone to consign to the glue-works and

* In a dubious tribute to their instigator, French rubbish bins would become known as *les poubelles*.

which might go to make buttons. Metal wasn't just metal, but tin, iron, copper, brass. And a composite thing like an old toothbrush would be broken down and its parts—bone handle, bristles, thread—sorted accordingly. By the end of the century, the sorters would be plucking bits of elastic from stocking tops for re-use in the manufacture of pneumatic tyres.

Chiffoniers, the bin-scavengers, struggled to make a living following the restrictive ordinance of 1883. A handful took jobs as municipal street-sweepers, but many more became, effectively, employees of the master ragpickers. There were some, though, who kept their independence by selling their gleanings at a scrap market in the suburbs that would become known as *marché aux puces*, literally 'market with fleas'—the original flea market.*

In the twentieth century garbage-scouring would become the province of big business and organised crime. In New York at the end of World War II, three firms—master rag-pickers, in effect—paid the city for 'combing rights' that yielded millions of dollars a year. Garbage collected by the Department of Sanitation was loaded on barges that would stand at dock while 'field workers' combed their contents for items of value, mainly

* For more on flea markets, see chapter 18.

recyclables. After twenty-four hours, tugs towed the barges to shallow water or swampy ground, where the garbage was dumped to extend the city shoreline. There, thousands more combers—freelancers—would swarm over it, finding a livelihood in second pickings.

Waste wasn't waste while a use could still be found for it. In later chapters we'll see how the idea of waste would change as economies came increasingly to rely on accelerating the obsolescence of things. There *is* such a thing as waste, it turns out, and affluence produces it.

CHAPTER 6

Destitute of Apparel

Could not some means be adopted of collecting some of the left-off clothes, with shoes, &c.... so as to clothe the naked and keep the bare foot from the cold floor?

HENRY WARREN OF ADELAIDE, 1885

In Victorian Britain and throughout the progress-minded world, the ranks of 'the respectable' continued to grow. To them, second-hand was on the nose—and not just for themselves. The working poor, it was felt, should aspire to dress in cheap ready-made. Never mind the quality; what mattered was that it was new. Female servants who took pleasure in wearing their mistresses' 'quickly-cast-off fashionable clothing', given them as perks, were condemned as sluttish—

> *I ask you whether any observant person can walk the streets of our cities or towns on Sundays* [servants' one day off] *without feelings of pity and disgust?… kitchen and scullery maids, aping the absurdities of their superiors in station, with lace or make-believe lace petticoats, crinolines, kid gloves, parasols, and preposterous head dresses.*

If wearing clothing of the right sort preserved moral order, a veneration of *new* proved that one had—literally—bought into progress, the locomoting imperative of the nineteenth-century world.

And for the first time ever there were germs to worry about. Not that there hadn't been germs before, but with progress in science came a clearer picture of what they did and where they might lurk. As long ago as 1665, a bale of cast-off clothes brought from London had been blamed for introducing bubonic plague to a remote Derbyshire village.

Until about 1870, though, if second-hand clothing carried a taint, it was the social one of downward mobility. Spreading as the nineteenth century did, that taint essentially reversed the class connotations of second-hand clothes. Before that, for the longest time, there was satisfaction, even pride, in wearing a garment for which someone of a higher station had once paid a pretty price. Certainly, writers found a rich seam of pathos—'How the mighty have fallen!'—in speculating over the past lives of a Rag Fair garment.

Cue germ theory, though, and fantasies about previous wearers were no longer so benign. Tuberculosis, scarlet fever, typhus, smallpox, even cancer—who knew what contagion a cast-off might harbour? New laws would mandate disinfection, fumigation. Even so, the second-hand trade seemed surely doomed. Who, besides the rag mills, would have old clothing now? Well, the poor. Specifically the deserving poor, as second-hand became increasingly the stuff of charity.

The work of missionaries had long depended on donations of cast-off clothing. The South Sea Mission, in 1839, had assured Sydney donors 'that any articles, however much worn and apparently useless, would be received by the natives with gladness and would be a step towards their civilisation'. An appeal to 'the well-to-do people of Adelaide' for their cast-offs, on the other hand, aimed more frankly to shield white children on the Coorong from 'the present naked state of the blacks [which] is both demoralising and disgustingly indecent'.

The very poorest—those unable to support themselves—relied on the charities that proliferated over the course of the nineteenth century as towns and cities grew and social gulfs widened. Benevolent societies and urban missions gave assistance to widows, single mothers, the infirm and the aged. But that assistance was usually meagre and contingent: soup, a penny or two, a bed for a night, an assurance of salvation in the hereafter. The diary kept by a city missionary during Melbourne's boom era records that it was no uncommon thing to find, in a back-lane shanty, a starving, workless family without a stick of furniture or a pair of shoes between them. Typically their pious visitor could only make whatever utterance 'seemed best' and offer a religious tract or two.

Charities were slow to recognise, or at least to articulate, the importance of clothing to their charges' wellbeing. But without decent coverings, a man couldn't seek work or his children attend school. (If anyone had to go shoeless, the thinking went, best it be the mother.) Charities encouraged church attendance as a route to self-improvement, yet rags were hardly fitting for the Lord's house. After a group of charity cases was shepherded to church in London one Sunday, an appeal went out—

> *As the apparel of these poor people was in a deplorable condition, the Committee will feel grateful for the present of any cast-off clothing, in order that they may be enabled to attend Divine service in future with greater comfort, decency and propriety.*

Country clergymen in England were so poorly paid as to be themselves in need of charity. The Poor Clergy Relief Society took donations on their behalf, of clothing as well as money. 'My only suit of clothes is threadbare,' wrote one curate in supplication, 'and I have no shoes to my feet.' Another told of having travelled to a distant town to buy second-hand clothes incognito. Even so, 'It is a degradation that I have painfully felt.'

Calls for donations of old clothes tended to be sporadic and seasonal, and for the benefit of institutional inmates—of asylums, hospitals, orphanages—rather than for distribution among the poor at large. There was the old suspicion that donated items would be sold to buy booze, as well as the question (not unrelated) of who was deserving and who was not. The institutionalised poor qualified; for those on the outside, the designation was muddier.

'It is only a common act of Christian charity to clothe the naked,' wrote a commentator in Adelaide in winter 1852. Yet although the Destitute Board, tasked with supplying 'outdoor relief' to the poor, received many requests for cast-off clothing, 'no such contributions have ever been received'. The writer implored the benevolent to donate 'articles of left-off attire' and bedding which would, they were assured, be 'distributed with carefulness'—meaning, only to the truly deserving.

That people rarely gave old clothes to charity is evident from the fact that such donors would be individually acknowledged—by name or else anonymously—in the newspapers.

> *The Committee beg to express their thanks to* [among others]*...an 'Old Friend', for several suits of clothes...—two distressed literary gentlemen have in consequence been amply provided with clothing.*
>
> *...the Ladies' Committee...beg to acknowledge a bag of cast-off clothing from Mrs Shipton...*
>
> *...the committee expressed their gratitude for a box of left-off clothing, the gift of G. B. Cuthbert, Esq., a good example which they hope may be followed.*

This reluctance of the otherwise benevolent was attributed by some to the perennial fear of their former garments being recognised on the backs of paupers. Then there were the servants to consider: 'Your old housekeeper [will] be seriously vexed if you attempt to rob her of her perquisites.'

Exceptions were made, apparently, in cases of wholesale (rather than individual) calamity, particularly if such calamity occurred at a safe distance from the donor. In 1836 British abolitionists amassed a cargo of cast-offs to clothe 387 would-have-been slaves shipwrecked off Grenada. During the Lancashire 'cotton famine' of the early 1860s the benevolent, from London to the far reaches of the Empire, were appealed to for clothing to aid the families of mill-workers whose livelihood was lost. (Among the hundreds of bales collected, there was the usual assortment of misfits: ball dresses, white tulle bonnets, silver-buckled dress shoes.) Old clothing was in constant demand during the American Civil War and afterwards, for freed slaves and 'contrabands', prisoners of war and others left destitute on both sides of the ragged front. Even in the event of a grasshopper plague (Kansas, 1874), the call would go out: 'Ladies, ransack the wardrobes around your house.'

Perhaps all this faceless benevolence in answer to distant calamities had the effect of softening people to the idea of giving at home. Or perhaps, 'in our modern times, when garments are affairs of a few months', they simply had more to give. Perhaps servants could more readily afford to dress in new garments. And—no *perhaps* here—the stigma of disease and opprobrium had knocked the bottom out of the second-hand trade. For a host of reasons, by the late 1880s the charitable giving of cast-off clothes flowed freely. Just as well, since the Great Depression was about to make landfall.

In Australia, the Society of St Vincent de Paul typified the large-scale operations that arose to meet the distress of the 1890s.* Founded in Paris sixty years earlier, the society had recognised from the start that 'the poor are as often in want of clothes as of food' and so appointed a

* Internationally, outfits like the Salvation Army and Goodwill took relief operations to another level—see chapter 9 for an account of their role in the evolution of op shops.

Keeper of the Wardrobe in each chapter. The Melbourne chapter, in the 1890s, had its wardrobe—really a storehouse—tended by a legion of female volunteers who cleaned and mended garments for distribution. A tally was kept and published of the number of garments and pairs of boots given out each year. For 1897, that tally was 886 and 139 respectively, which seems modest for a population of more than 450,000. True, the society was a Catholic charity in a city split along sectarian lines. Yet it's clear that, even given the 'modern times', clothes weren't cast off with anything like the profligacy of *our* times.

An appeal went out to 'the Well Inclined' in the country districts: 'There is a great deal of poverty and distress in the suburbs of Melbourne; in many cases people are starving and without clothes...it is found [that] disused clothing, boots and shoes are very acceptable to the deserving poor.' At the Brotherhood Mission in North Melbourne, 'Any description of left-off clothing would be a great boon, as many come to us whose clothing is so bad that they cannot hope to be employed anywhere.' Appealing to 'those possessed of this world's goods' with assurances of 'a fumigator in full blast', the Brotherhood missionary prayed 'that they may not shut the bowels of their compassion'.*

* In fact the Bible credits the bowels as the seat of one's tender emotions, evoking the evergreen pastime of shitting on the poor.

The patron saint of the poor was St Martin who tore his cloak in half to share with a beggar in a snowstorm. Some churches marked his annual feast, 11 November, with Ol' Clo' Sunday, taking up a collection of cast-offs; but the spirit in which such gifts were solicited often seemed contrary to the spirit of the saint. Under the headline 'HELPING THE POOR', a Sydney newspaper tempered its call for Christian charity thus:

> *Of course, the kindest little hands could never make a silk frock serviceable or suitable for such wearers, but out-grown coats, worn under-garments, and the boys' cast-off clothes would be far more welcome and useful than treble their money value. Paradoxical as it may seem, it is through their small value that they are so valuable. It is no temptation to the most degraded, drunken father or mother to pawn or sell what would hardly fetch the price of one of their favourite drinks.*

It's not surprising then that the spirit in which goods were given could be less than charitable. A journalist who witnessed the opening of parcels sent to a Sydney charity wrote that 'we were not sure whether to laugh or be angry'—

> *There were dresses of good material so hopelessly dirty that they were only fit to be burnt. There were garments from which the thrifty owners had*

> *removed every hook and eye, and every button. There were...shoes worn through the soles, men's felt hats soaking in grease and dirt, odd stockings riddled with holes...*

More—far more—than half the goods received were dirty and beyond repair, and it was plain that 'To give them as charity was an easy way of disposing of rubbish which ought to have gone under the copper'—to have been burnt, in other words.

West Australians, it seems, were generous with their old clothes. A decade after the 1895 gold rush to Western Australia, the Goldfields Football Association set up a left-off clothing department to aid indigent men in Kalgoorlie, most of them miners out of work and luck, who were revered as 'pioneers'. Margaret Bale, a teacher from Kalgoorlie, made a genuinely pioneering use of such largesse. In 1909 she took a train to Perth and shed both clothes and identity on Cottesloe Beach. Exchanging a brown Holland skirt, cream-coloured blouse, white straw hat and veil for a tweed suit and hat and a pair of blucher boots, he regained the street as Martin Able, but not before burying 'a quantity of troublesome lingerie' in the sand. The rest of his female attire he wrapped in brown paper and sent by post to a charitable body in Fremantle.

Besides giving aid to gold-rush pioneers, Aborigines and dwellers in their own dockside slums, Westralians were both well inclined and well placed—being two thousand kilometres (some weeks by sea) nearer than most Australians—to send speedy relief to the London poor and Europe's wartime refugees. In particular, tens of thousands of Belgians, displaced by the German invasion in 1914, who had only the clothes they stood up in. But West Australian loyalties were torn. When an appeal was launched in Perth the local chapter of the National Council of Women protested: 'When the people in this State are provided for, then whatever is over can be sent to Belgium.'*

For many of the State's farmers and rural settlers were also in distress. From the 1890s, settlers had been encouraged to develop the outlying districts collectively known as the wheatbelt, but drought and broken promises had reduced farming families to desperation. All the same, they resented being cast as charity cases by the 'well-meaning busybodies' at the NCW. 'Cast-off clothing for the women of the bush! Not one farmer's wife or daughter in a hundred would accept such gifts.' Indeed, one such wife declared she'd rather go naked; another told a Perth newspaper—

> *No doubt they meant well, but is it a fair thing to ask their less fortunate sisters to come down to*

* Frustration would continue, during and after the First World War, that 'quite a lot of useful gifts' were diverted from the home front to refugees and influenza victims abroad.

> *that level? No; we do not want their left-off things. No woman with any spirit would accept such an indignity.*

That's how it could go when fortunes changed, mashing up notions of 'deserving' and 'respectable'. Twenty years later, during the Depression, a Parramatta woman with six children and a husband out of work had to rely on the cast-offs of strangers. 'I hate charity,' she confided to the Sydney *Truth*—

> *It reminds me of when I was a child, the blacks were given blankets once a year. Little did I think then we would come to the same pass.*

It had long been recognised, by those willing to see (or with no choice), that having to accept others' cast-offs might 'obtrude on the mind of the recipient a sense of asserted superiority'. 'Can you tell me,' asked a woman who volunteered at a sewing guild, in 1936—

> *why it is that so many people who give their left-off clothing to charities pull off all tapes, buttons, pyjama cords, and linings out of coats?...Those poor unfortunates who receive these old clothes should not be made to feel that buttons, tapes, etc., are too good for them.*

Many families were humbled during the 1930s by experiencing for the first time a dependence on charity.

And not just charity, but begging. Addressing readers of the 'Woman to Woman' page in the *Weekly Times*, 'Alone' wrote: 'My husband is in a mental home, and I would be very glad of some left-off clothing for myself and little girls, one year and nine years, or anything to cut down.' 'Jonquil', wife of an invalid and mother of seven, insisted that 'I am not asking for charity'—

> *but if any of your readers have any left-off clothing to fit boys of 13, 10, 8 and 2 years respectively, and girls of 12 and 6, and a baby boy of 12 months, I would be only too pleased to pay a reasonable price for same, especially footwear, as that is the greatest problem in our district.*

Outside of the cities, second-hand clothing in Australia was practically unprocurable *except* as charity. And even in town, charitable giving had substantially reduced the availability of used clothing to those who could afford to buy. In perception if not actuality, second-hand and charity had become almost indivisible—at least where clothing was concerned.

Voices in the leftist press were as scornful and repudiative of charitable cast-offs as West Australian farmers' wives had been, only cursing different oppressors: namely, capitalism and 'the parasite class'—

> *...the day is coming when the people of sweat and*

> *sorrow will refuse to [accept] your cast-off clothing and blankets; they will rise in a mighty army and take that which your class has held back from them by fraud.*
>
> *The capitalists rob us in their industries and then come and preach to us and give us their left-off clothing...Sweet charity. Oh, hell!*

The tone had changed, but these diatribes from the Sydney *Workers' Weekly* echoed a sentiment voiced by Henry Mayhew in his survey of the London poor eighty years earlier. Noting (approvingly) that a poor woman with just a penny to spare might buy her little girl a petticoat at a street stall, Mayhew went on—

> *But whether the state of things in which an industrious widow...can spare but a penny for a child's clothing (and nothing, perhaps, for their own), is one to be lauded in a Christian country, is [a] question, fraught with grave political and social considerations.*

In the next century, American political theorist Michael Harrington would conclude, the poor didn't disappear but were made less visible: 'The affluent society [had] given out costumes to the poor so that they would not offend the rest of society with the sight of rags.'

CHAPTER 7

Her Superfluous Fal-lals

To wear a dress out is an achievement no woman aspires to in these days of love of change.

FREMANTLE MAIL, 1905

Pushed to the margins by shoddy and charity, the second-hand clothes trade reverted for the most part to being women's business. By the turn of the twentieth century, you'd hear more of ol' clo' *women* than men. In the poorer parts of any city there would be women who, knowing their neighbours' needs and wants and situations, would procure second-hand things—at pawnbrokers' auctions and charity sales, or from whoever was selling—with particular buyers in mind. The tailored brokerage of an ol' clo' woman saved her neighbours the shame of being seen shopping for second-hand themselves or, worse, of resorting to charity.

In fact, there were—perhaps always had been—dealers who offered a discreet, personalised service in the second-hand line not just to the poor, but at all social levels. In eighteenth-century Paris it was the *revendeuse à la toilette* who was 'in the confidence of the finest ladies' and could be relied upon to find a ready buyer for luxury goods in the event of, say, a gambling debt. 'Women such as this only exist in Paris,' wrote a contemporary commentator.

Yet the circumstance in which even a wealthy woman might lack access to cash or credit without her husband's knowledge was far from uncommon in 1870s New York, or Sydney after Federation. The imperative to be 'in the fashion' tugged ever more insistently at the sleeves of women up and down the social ladder. The modes shed at the top would be in demand from those just below—and so there remained a good living to be made as a dealer in 'discarded finery'. She was equally valued by seller and buyer, supplying the one with cash towards her next ensemble and the other with affordable near-la-modes (as well as pecuniary consolation to the new widow whose 'flaringly fashionable wardrobe' was rendered suddenly obsolete).

Top-end finery would usually find a buyer just half a rung down, one who was in the social swim but insufficiently cashed-up for first-wear couture. Unfailing discretion on the dealer's part was essential, as 'no lady likes to be caught selling off her dresses' and it would never do for a new owner to have her outfit recognised as second-hand. As subterfuge, a garment might be restyled or re-trimmed before selling-on, or else transplanted to fresh social territory. A leading New York dealer of the early 1870s ('a shrewd old Frenchwoman') also operated in Boston, circulating her acquisitions between the two cities.* Sydney and Melbourne society wore each other's cast-offs, as well as London's. And pre-worn Paris fashions could be worn anywhere with not just impunity but pride.

With the new century, quality second-hand attracted a new level of respectability. 'To wear a dress out is an achievement no woman aspires to in these days of love of change.' Not only were fashions changing faster, but 'the craze for "suitability"', as it was dubbed by a writer in *The Boudoir, An Illustrated Magazine for Gentlewomen*, meant one must have *more* outfits at one's disposal. 'The mere acceptance of a drive in a motor-car,' wrote Mrs Jack Johnson, 'necessitates an equipment beyond the purse of the average human being.' Even 'gentlewomen by birth' openly patronised 'dress agencies' that sold clothes euphemised as 'misfits'. 'The "ole clo"' lady is now no old

* The social elite of New York at the time was termed 'The 400': the number denoted the capacity of Mrs Astor's ballroom.

nagging harridan, but a smiling, amiable, well-dressed woman, who shows her wares in a nice, clean, up-to-date shop, where no one need fear to enter.'

Another writer purported to trace a scarcely worn 'hundred-guinea gown' to just such an establishment, where it sold for quarter its original price. Even the finest undergarments, so costly new, were sold there second-hand. 'It is a boon to the woman who is obliged to dress handsomely and has only a limited amount of pin money on which to do so, to be able to go to these places without loss of caste.' But dealers in second-hand finery, it was rumoured, also enjoyed the custom of the demi-monde. There was nothing new in that: Mayhew had noted, fifty years earlier, that prostitutes ('who required some further protection from the night air') were among the best customers of a particular dealer in second-hand furs. But in 1905 Sydney, 'precautions are taken'—by sending garments interstate for resale—'that the society lady is not likely to be offended by the sight of her cast-off spring costume or evening gown on a woman of no importance'.

Conversely, a singer at London's Alhambra Theatre who costumed herself in titled ladies' cast-offs posed 'A Question about Low Dresses' to readers of the *Pall Mall Gazette*: how was it that a ballgown previously worn by a duchess was considered too indecent for the stage? The refined dress agencies of New York and London were much patronised by young singers and actresses. 'It is an unwritten law among them that they must...always [be] in the very van of fashion, decking themselves with what is the very latest cry.' Though lowly paid, journeyman performers were expected to look their best on-stage and off, and even to supply their own costumes. In London, the Theatrical Ladies' Guild ran a cast-off clothing department. 'And there isn't an actress or an actor who applies,' said one of the organisers, 'that we cannot find the very things they need for the part they are engaged to play.' The great actress Ellen Terry was a donor, as were 'crowds of other well-known people'.

From the *fin de siècle* to the Great War, Paris was the undisputed capital of prestige second-hand. American tourists shopped there for cast-offs of a calibre rarely seen at home, and so did dealers like Olivia Sanborn of New York, whom agents in Paris and throughout Europe supplied with the discards of society women and nobility, even royalty. Selling 'the cast-off clothes of Royalty' was the specialty of at least one Paris *revendeuse*. Americans were her keenest customers, she said, as 'they regard Royalty with worship'.

Olivia Sanborn was a case in point: she'd been a collector before she was a dealer, and had graced society balls dressed entirely in the cast-offs of royalty. According to one London dealer, fraud was rife in this rarefied market, since a cloak of 'discretion' easily obscured the real origins of costumes claimed as royal.

In earlier times, the cast-off clothes of royalty had typically gone to their servants as a pretty perk, possibly in lieu of wages. That was still the practice in some parts of Europe, with the maidservant of Italy's Dowager Queen reportedly making the equivalent of £1,000 a year from the sale—to Americans, mostly—of her mistress's cast-offs. At the same period in Spain, King Alfonso's cast-offs were sold annually, with the proceeds used to defray part of his clothing budget for the year ahead. Kaiser Wilhelm's clothes were sold for charitable purposes, while Tsar Nicholas II gave his ordinary clothes as perks to his valets but let his uniforms and furs be sold for the benefit of 'poorer people about the Court'.

In England, before he assumed the throne as Edward VII in 1901, the Prince of Wales was viewed askance for hoarding his discarded clothes. He'd buy no fewer than eight suits at once and wear each just four times. Rather than allowing his cast-offs as perks to his valet, as per convention, he stored them—thousands of suits of clothing—at Marlborough House in what were called the 'brushing rooms', with several men employed to care for them. His successor, George V, would have his old uniforms sold to benefit charities, while the rest of the royal household's clothing was given to the poor, 'in such a way, however, that they do not know to whom the clothes belonged'.

Talk of clothes and royalty inevitably harks back to the regent from whom the Regency got its name: George IV, the dandy king. It was, in part, his mammoth debts to tailors and outfitters that forced his marriage to the well-heeled Caroline of Brunswick. Years later, estranged from the vain and corpulent king, Queen Caroline would jeer: 'He understands how a shoe should be made or a coat cut...and would make an excellent tailor, or shoemaker or hairdresser but nothing else.' Like Edward VII after him, George hoarded his cast-offs. These, though, were no ordinary suits of clothing, but sumptuous and bejewelled, a trove of foppish finery.

Upon his death in 1830, 'His late Majesty's costly and splendid wardrobe' was sold at auction, with the proceeds going as perks to servants and dependants of the royal household. Lasting a fortnight, the auction raised just £15,000, a tiny fraction of what George must have outlaid. (Consider that, thirty-five years earlier, his tailors' bill alone had stood at more than £30,000.) The late sovereign's crimson velvet coronation mantle, embroidered lavishly with gold, fetched just one-tenth of the £500 it had cost and would end up on display at Madame Tussaud's. His coronation ruff, of superb Mechlin lace, was knocked down at £2, and a pair of satin-lined kid trousers ('of ample dimensions') at just twelve shillings.* Hundreds of pairs of bespoke shoes, buckled and fallaled, went for five shillings a pair. 'There was,' noted *The Times*, 'very slight competition for any of the articles and we did not observe that they were knocked down to persons of distinction.' But whoever the *actual* buyers were, every second-hand trader in London would, for months to come, have touted some portion of their wares as having come from 'the great sale' and asked a penny or two more as the price of prestige.†

Another kind of prestige imbued the five cassocks cast off annually by Pope Pius IX. Even though their vestal whiteness was yellowed by the Pope's constant snuff-taking, they—along with the papal slippers, changed monthly—were highly prized by the moneyed faithful.

Following Abraham Lincoln's assassination, many of his effects were given as keepsakes to friends and White House retainers. The late president's messenger received a cane and some treasured items of apparel, while a 'shepherd plaid shawl…which was rendered somewhat

* A pair of George IV's breeches still extant has a waist circumference of nearly 1.4 metres.

† Speaking of finery, not long after the sale of George IV's, an ol' clo' dealer found, sewn into the lining of a tattered velvet dress, a bank draft for two thousand francs and a letter of introduction dated 1792, citing the nameless bearer's 'misfortunes, rank and virtues'. The suggestion was that the dress had belonged to Marie Antoinette.

memorable as forming part of his famous disguise, together with the Scotch cap, when he wended his way secretly to the Capitol to be inaugurated' went to a friend in Canada. The hat last worn by Lincoln was given to the clergyman who was with him when he died. A point was made that 'not an article was parted with for money'. Two years later, however, Lincoln's hard-up widow, Mary, put her First Lady wardrobe up for sale. Twenty-five dresses, together with shawls, furs and jewellery, on display at an agent's office on Broadway, presented an attraction for 'the curious and speculative'—

> *The feeling of the majority of visitors is adverse to the course Mrs Lincoln has thought proper to pursue, and the criticisms are as severe as the cavillings are persistent at the quality of some of the dresses...they are jagged under the arms and at the bottom of the skirt, stains are on the lining...*

Considering their condition and that they had 'passed out of fashion', general opinion was that the dresses were overpriced. Also, they were strikingly décolleté, a 'peculiarity' attributed to 'Mrs Lincoln's appreciation of her own bust'. Her White House stylist and confidante, Elizabeth Keckley,* protested to the *Evening News* 'that the Empress

* Keckley had kept as mementos clothes worn by Mrs Lincoln on 'that fatal night', including a velvet cloak 'completely bespattered with blood'.

of France frequently disposes of her cast-off wardrobe, and publicly too, without being subjected to any unkind remarks regarding its propriety'. Why might widowed Mary Todd Lincoln not claim the same immunity? As First Lady, she had gained a reputation for extravagance which, while not a pip on George IV's, continued to sour the press and public against her—and her frocks.

One day near the end of his life, the poet and essayist Ralph Waldo Emerson was confronted at home by 'a tall female' wanting some of his clothes. She was making a 'poets rug'—a patchwork quilt, presumably—of poets' cast-offs sewn together. Henry Wadsworth Longfellow had given her an old shirt; now she was hoping for a pair of Emerson's worn-out trousers. More prosaic (yet poetic in its way) was the manner by which a workman came into, then lost, possession of a suit belonging to an Australian prime minister. Hired as a rouseabout at Billy Hughes's residence in 1918, the man was issued as his work gear, by *Mrs* Hughes, a shabby old suit of her husband's. But the suit, it turned out, was the prime minister's favourite and he demanded it back. The rouseabout was consoled by one of Hughes's political opponents that 'You should be a proud man, for the prime minister is wearing your cast-off clothing.'

As the twentieth century went celluloid, the unwanted clothing and effects of dead, distressed or opportunistic celebrities would find an ever-ready market. Barbara Stanwyck's high heels, a tailored suit of Joan Crawford's, Hedy Lamarr's brassiere, Lana Turner's girdle: an establishment called Gowns of the Stars on Hollywood's Sunset Strip bought them direct from the 'film queens' and in bulk from the studios, then sold them for about one-fifth of their original value. Later, Julien's in Los Angeles would make its name as auctioneer to the stars, knocking down at stratospheric prices such modern icons as Marilyn Monroe's 'Happy Birthday, Mr President' dress, Michael Jackson's white glove and a polo shirt worn by James Gandolfini as Tony Soprano.

Now, James Stewart—*he* was my kind of movie star. In London in 1950 for the filming of 'No Highway in the Sky', the lanky actor searched in vain for a convincingly shabby suit to wear in his role as an eccentric scientist. 'It's no use trying to fake this sort of thing in the costume department,' he despaired. 'The suit has to be genuinely worn to look right.'* He did have one suit that fit the bill, but he'd already worn it in half a dozen movies (including the big-rabbit classic, *Harvey*) and: 'I guess the public may be getting tired of it'. What Stewart needed was a jumble sale.

* I know what you're thinking, but forget it. Even given a time machine, that shabby suit of Billy Hughes's (1.68 m tall) would've been no use whatever to Jimmy Stewart (1.9 m).

CHAPTER 8

Enough Humility to Wear a Rummage Hat

The jumbling at the stacked trestle tables got underway in earnest.

AGE (MELBOURNE), 1979

Those well-off Potts Pointers and brownstone-dwellers who, around the turn of the twentieth century, sold their cast-off finery to dealers were liable to be castigated in the press for not giving it to charity instead. In their defence, it was argued that clothing of the kind they wore was 'entirely unfitted to the uses of their poorer sisters'. But there was a way to benefit charity *and* find suitable homes for their classy duds: give them to a jumble sale.

Before jumble came rummage. The word *rummage* (related to *room*) originally referred to the arrangement of cargo in a ship's hold.* Once in port, damaged or unclaimed cargo would be offered in a rummage sale. A typical rummage sale held on London's West India Docks early in Victoria's reign might clear several tons of mahogany, as well as wine and spirits, sperm candles† and leftover ship's provisions. But the name was taken up in the US around 1858 to describe a new kind of local fundraiser, selling donated handicrafts, garden produce and unwanted household goods, including clothing. Rummage sales caught on during the Civil War, as they enabled women who lacked money of their own to contribute to the cause—*and* to buy second-hand clothes from a reputable source. The shame of proximity to a garment's original owner would have been offset by the virtuous glow cast by thrift in a time of privation.

It would take about thirty years for rummage sales to cross the Atlantic. In 1891, in a town just outside London, an 'American Fair or Rummage Sale' was announced, in aid of the Congregational Sunday school. The idea was so novel as to require an explanation:

> *The peculiarity of the Rummage Sale is that nothing new is sold, but all the articles are second hand, contributed by friends, who presumably have*

* As a verb, *rummage* can mean either to stow closely or to ransack.

† Candles made from the oil of sperm whales.

'rummaged' their houses for all the old or disused things they can find.

Among middle-class and working people, especially those living outside cities, second-hand clothing had become all but un-gettable, except within families as hand-me-downs. The very poor might come by it as charity, and the social elites had their sources of slightly used finery. But the stigma of second-hand had collapsed the market and put it out of reach of many ordinary folk. As we've seen, even clergymen struggled to keep themselves decently clad. In an age of Shanks's pony, elbow grease and the mangle, clothing and footwear were worn hard and when bought new were still costly in proportion to wages. How was a mother, no matter how thrifty, to keep her family in shoe leather and broadcloth?

Her desperation partly accounts for the terrific and immediate success of rummage sales—which, within just a few years, were more likely to be called, in Britain and its dependencies, *jumble* sales instead. Right from the start, no report of a sale held, say, to buy a classroom piano or pay off a hall debt would fail to mention the alacrity with which the stock sold out. 'When the doors were opened there was a great crush,' and, 'Although advertised to be held on Saturday as well as Friday, the sale proceeded with such unexpected rapidity that the large collection of miscellaneous goods was almost entirely disposed of before 6 o'clock on the first day.' It was not unheard of for three hundred people or more to cram into a schoolroom where a jumble sale was at full pitch.

The rise of the jumble sale coincided with a growing sense among the philanthropic that charity was degrading and that their gifts were met with resentment. A jumble sale, with goods given free and priced for quick sale, gave agency even to a buyer with just pennies to spend. Even though the stuff for sale was second-hand, there was pleasure in being a shopper instead of a supplicant—not to mention the thrill of a bargain.

> *When one sees a crowd of ill-clad women with suit cases and sugar bags wending their way in subdued excitement to a hall in the afternoon, one may be pretty certain that a jumble sale is there...With a scant purse and a high hope, each one of the genuine poor enters...*

A jumble sale sold whatever it was given—'files of the *Girl's Own Paper*, decrepit bassinettes, hymn books, saucepans and feeding bottles'—but the greatest demand was for old clothes. A study of the working poor in York at the turn of the twentieth century found that women would save up all year, scrimping a pittance from each week's housekeeping, for their 'annual jumble sale dress'. In one of Melbourne's poorer suburbs, likewise, 'mothers save up for months for these sales, and look forward to fitting out themselves and their families there'.

There was a fad in the newspapers' women's pages, for a time, for short stories with titles like 'The Success of Our Rummage Sale', threaded with humorous riffs on the meanness of the rich and the ingratitude of the poor.

> *Mother looked up from the bundle of old hats which had just arrived at the vicarage. They represented all that my wealthy Aunt Alice and my cousins could do to help us in our rummage sale…'How hateful all one's rich relations always are,' I burst out. 'Mean brutes! I believe they sell all their things to old clo' women…Have you asked the Whites?'*
>
> *'Yes—two pairs of stockings with the heels worn off, and a silk petticoat which rends if you look at it too long.'*

'At any rate,' consoled the narrator's mother, 'the poor people are pleased, though they would die rather than say so.' This was hers and her daughter's seventh jumble sale, so they knew what to expect—

> *At 8 o'clock a large gathering of village folk invaded the schoolroom and began, with many disparaging remarks, to turn over and to cheapen the piles of miscellaneous clothing and effects.*
>
> *'I'll take that skirt, mum, if it ain't above a shilling. Good money for it, too; it's terribly worn*

> *around the edge, and driggledy-draggledy too.'*
>
> *'Could I have them three blouses for ninepence, miss? They're cruel old-fashioned. I mind your wearing one of them last summer...'*

Generally speaking, hats seem to have been among the most despised commodities at a jumble sale (hence, the scorn directed at 'the bundle of old hats' sent in by the rich relatives). There had been a time when a woman's hat would be interminably re-trimmed and renovated from season to season. Now, though, fashions changed too much, too fast; and at a jumble sale, hats vastly outnumbered buyers of hats. There'd likely be 'a large collection' of women's old straw hats selling at just a ha'penny each. Men's tall silk hats, too, were hard to shift.

In a story by US author Mary Stewart Cutting, a respectable woman of modest means, sorting donated goods in preparation for a rummage sale, agonises over whether to buy a hat she finds among them—

> *...if it were not a rummage hat! But what if it were? Would anyone know?...of course, you didn't know who had worn it before, but there was a subtle odour of violet about it that was reassuring.*

What the reader knows, but she doesn't, is that the hat had been worn just once by a well-to-do lady, whose servant sent it to the sale in error. In the end, for twenty-five cents, the conflicted buyer becomes its proud owner. 'And she was so glad that she had enough humility herself to wear a rummage hat!'

Likewise, at the Sydney free kindergarten's jumble sale, in 1908. 'It was a fine lesson in humility,' wrote a journalist who was there, 'to see a woman with a pinched, careworn face gaze longingly at a blouse marked sixpence, and then with a shake of the head move sadly away.' For sixpence, some buyers had gained early entry to the jumble sale and 'the pick of the bargains'. Donated goods had been sent in from 'the four corners of Sydney', but most of the buyers lived close by in the dockside streets of Woolloomooloo. From a little further afield came those who could afford 'silk and satin blouses at two shillings' and 'tailor-made coats and skirts at five shillings'. One, after paying for her purchases, still had two shillings and sixpence to spend on a floral hat, 'which, she announced with much dignity, was a present for a friend on the west coast of Tasmania.' (A likely story.)

> *There are countless odds and ends, such as old cashmere or woollen stockings, woollen underwear that only requires a little energy to renovate, the cast-off little dresses, coats and underclothing that the children have outgrown, and that inestimable boon to the poor—old boots.*

Girls' dresses were priced from sixpence to ninepence, children's suits cost a shilling, plain blouses between sixpence and a shilling, men's trousers and vests from one penny to sixpence, and shirts thruppence. 'The purchasing power of a penny was enormous', buying perhaps 'three pairs of stockings; a pair of gloves; three men's collars or six neckties'. When, after two hours, the jumble sale stalls were empty and around £15* had been raised, the organisers were said to be 'mightily pleased. They were doing a woman's work by helping other women'—to dress themselves and their families affordably—'and the profits would go to educate the children of those same women.'

A properly run jumble sale, then, gave twice. But when the goods on sale included donations from the better suburbs, there was sure to be a dealer or two among the early birds. In a way, it was only fair, since jumble sales surely eroded the business of the neighbourhood ol' clo' woman. But it was considered unsporting, particularly when a dealer, 'pathetic of countenance, eagle-eyed and badly dressed, tries to beat down to their lowest possible minimum the articles she can sell again so well'.

By the 1920s and '30s, people were getting accustomed to giving away, rather than selling or storing, their redundant stuff. It wasn't just that clothing fashions took

* A jumble sale 'engineered' by the Working Women's Guild at Geelong during the First World War made that amount in just forty-nine minutes.

radical turns, making replacement more viable than alteration; the arrival of modernity also drew a sharp line between new and old in décor, technology, hairstyles, entertainment—you name it. Jumble sales were among the beneficiaries.

> *Many and awesome were the rites and ceremonies by which the alchemists of old sought to transmute ordinary materials into gold. Turning unconsidered trifles into money is an art better understood to-day.*

(The event thus heralded was a 1927 jumble sale in Adelaide.)

> *Clothing of all kinds will be welcomed, also practically anything. The sad little ghosts of yesterday not wanted now, too good to throw away, taking up room and gathering dust in cupboards and on top shelves—where there still are top shelves, for the bungalows of to-day do not provide extensive attics for old furniture—these may find new homes and a fresh start in life.*

Those 'sad little ghosts' belonged to the category of jumble known as white elephant. When it first entered the parlance, just before the outbreak of the Great War, the white elephant stall—like *rummage* before it—needed some explaining. Ahead of one Red Cross jumble sale, it was reported that 'a misunderstanding regarding the

"White Elephant Stall" appears to exist', some donors picturing 'a stall for selling mascots or articles made up in the form of elephants'. What was sought, of course, were figurative white elephants: items for which householders no longer (and possibly never had) had a use.*

> *Who has not heard wife or husband say—'Confound that—(screen or gramophone, vase or jardinière)—it is always in the way!' This is the time to get it out of the way and turn it into cash and help for the soldiers; and possibly, to get it into a home where it will be a blessing.*

As had been the case during the American Civil War, women contributed to the war effort through patriotic drives, turning out cupboards and sheds for anything even nominally unwanted: 'the quaint comb bought in Colombo, the spears and boomerangs in the hall, the fan that belonged to grandmother, all disappear'. But within a very few years, holders of jumble sales were finding white elephant more a bugbear than a blessing. The alchemical principle, as applied to white elephants, held that exposure to the public gaze would reveal their worth; often, though, organisers were left with white elephants on

---

* The term was said to have originated with a *literal* rare white elephant, inflicted as a gift by a king of old Siam (Thailand) on a courtier he wished to ruin. It came to denote any gift that gave its recipient more trouble than it was worth.

their hands. Since the jumble-sale credo dictated that no donation may be refused, the most thoroughly irredeemable of them would be repurposed as lucky dips or given as prizes in quoit-throwing competitions.

Over the decades, jumble sales would themselves be restyled, as fêtes, car-boot sales, trash and treasure markets, and even domesticated as garage sales. For jumble-sale traditionalists, though, a classic venue—well into the 1980s—was Melbourne's lower town hall. The highlight of a Young Liberals jumble sale held there in 1965 was an assortment of items sent in by the soon-to-retire prime minister, Sir Robert Menzies: old classical records, neckties and Peter Cheyney thrillers. Best and biggest, though, was the annual Lady Mayoress's Fund jumble sale. The lady mayoress's squab-eating friends in the leafy suburbs would contribute their discarded finery—some of it disinterred from couture time capsules—which would go for a song to the shopper with the sharpest elbows. A committee member working the till at the 1979 jumble sale ruefully eyed a black cocktail dress. 'I would have liked to buy it,' she confessed, 'but if I wore it, someone would recognise it.'

CHAPTER 9

Silver Shoes for Sixpence

...it is intended to promote a scheme to be known as the 'opportunity shop'...

LADY MILLIE TALLIS, OCTOBER 1925

At Battersea, on the south side of the Thames, a huge sign appeared in 1891 announcing the DARKEST ENGLAND SALVAGE CONVERTOR. This was the brainchild of William Booth, founder of the Salvation Army, whose social-reform manifesto, *In Darkest England, and the Way Out*, had attracted worldwide notice the previous year. His chief idea was getting the poor to help themselves towards salvation, body and soul. To that end, his Army supplied a framework that encompassed worship, fellowship, food, shelter and work.

Among Booth's gifts as a master proselytiser was a talent for naming things. The Salvage Convertor was the depot of the Household Salvage Brigade, a waste-collection enterprise proposed in *Darkest England*. Brigade conscripts could find work by day and a bed at night in the Army's so-called 'elevators' wherein, by reclaiming waste goods for sale and recycling, 'the submerged'* might themselves be uplifted. Members of the Salvage Brigade, formerly destitute, received a token wage on top of board, lodging and uniform, and gained skills that might equip them for real employment.

Cartloads of pith helmets, worn (out) by British troops occupying Cairo in the 1880s, were sent by the War Office to the 'Darkest England' depot for salvage—leather straps went to the dyeworks, pith and cotton covering were consigned to manure.† More typically, rags and wastepaper were sorted, tin cans made into toys, old clothes cleaned and mended, umbrellas repaired and 'broken victuals' (food waste) became meals for the needy. By 1895, the Salvage Brigade was active in Australia: distributing bags house to house in the suburbs, to be filled with unwanted goods and left out for collection, sorting and sale.

---

* Booth also wrote and spoke of 'human wastage'.

† The earliest uniforms of the Salvation Army, even before it took that name, were cobbled together from old military ones.

The success of the Salvation Army's scheme for tackling 'the problem of the waste commodities of the towns' points to an increase in waste and reduced activity by salvage merchants since Mayhew's time. Indeed, in *Darkest England*, General Booth had waxed nostalgic for the itinerant rag-and-bone man and rued that 'luxurious living and thriftless habits have so increased'. As we have seen, taste and trade in second-hand were changing, as was the concept of charity. So that when, as an outgrowth of its waste-conversion enterprise, the Army began running salvage stores, selling old stuff for next to nothing, they found a ready market.

In 1908 the *War Cry* profiled the Army's salvage store in the northern city of Leeds, which opened twice a week, selling 'wastage from the homes of the wealthy'. An inventory of particulars included the invariable 'vast assortment of miscellaneous headgear for men' and 'heaps of umbrellas—most needing repair', as well as—

> *ladies' millinery; rolls of used linoleum; skirts, mantles, blouses, underwear, boots and shoes, dancing pumps and wellington boots...sponge and hip baths, a crippled sewing machine, a meat chopper, a mangle roller, perambulators, mail-carts and bassinets... glass and china ware, furniture both large and small, and even two useless firearms!*

The salvage store may have been synchronous with

the jumble sale, but it was industrial in scale and impulse where the jumble sale was genteel-amateur. And while a jumble sale lasted just an afternoon, a salvage store was forever. The Salvos may not actually have *invented* the charitable second-hand store (there were depots selling donated cast-offs to London's poor in the mid-1880s), but theirs was the model that others would imitate.

The Salvation Army had salvage brigades in major US cities from 1897, and Goodwill Industries kicked off in Boston in 1902. Like the Salvos, Goodwill (affiliated with the Methodist Church) ran a large-scale salvage and recycling enterprise. Its proud boast was that all items for sale in Goodwill stores had been disinfected and repaired, humble undertakings that were likened to God's work. A handbook for Goodwill workers offered departmental devotions such as these—

> *A Prayer for the Sorting and Pricing Room— Our Father... Give to our sorters and pricers wisdom to waste nothing and to see in each article whatever service can be rendered in Thee...*
>
> *A Prayer for the Repairing of Small Wares—... May the spirit of the master overflow in blessing to all who shall help to assemble these things and may these things like the dry bones in the Prophet's vision be so joined part to part that they shall live again in a career of blessing to others.*

But if repair work constituted the main occupation of Goodwill Industries, their chief *objective*—creating work for the disadvantaged and raising funds for its social programs—was still 'human salvage'.

Not so Vinnies. The Society of St Vincent de Paul, a charitable chapter of the Catholic Church, began its own salvage operations in London and several US cities in the early years of the twentieth century under the unlovely moniker of Waste Collection Bureaux. Unlike the Salvos and Goodwill, the mission of these bureaux was straight-up fundraising for the Society's good works, rather than work-as-salvation. They even had a slogan: 'Discarded by you—Treasured by others.'

It was 1922 before Waste Collection Bureaux reached Australia, but at that time Vinnie's had the field of charitable salvage to themselves because the Salvos' operations in that line had been halted by the First World War. In Sydney, the depot of the Waste Collection Bureau in Newtown accepted waste of all sorts, for recycle or resale. One week's donations, early on, included 'a cartload of furniture, another of timber and glass from a demolished building, a wire dummy such as is used by dressmakers, a bath, and a couple of wash-tubs'. Part of the depot served as a shop and—a sign that such a set-up was still novel to Australians—the press spruiked like a sideshow 'this extraordinary jumble of goods'—

> *Picture to yourself a large, barn-like shop...You will see piles of left-off clothing, both ladies' and gents', side by side with gas stoves; and in close proximity there are to be found Paris hats and perambulators, boots and invalid chairs, furniture and gas pipes, bathtubs and crockery, broken brass and carpenters' tools, umbrellas, ladies' bags, old paper, bottles, and tailors' cuttings—in fact there is hardly any conceivable article that ever was made which is not represented in this quaint old curiosity shop.*

Sometime early in the evolution of jumble sales and salvage stores, their target clientele had shifted from 'the needy' to just anyone. Charitable bodies selling second-hand had originally supposed that their only customers would be those unable to afford new. But there were people for whom even outright need couldn't overcome an aversion to second-hand, while it was plain that some others, poor and otherwise, were immune to the stigma. And so, pretty soon, the business model for charitable second-hand settled at selling cheaply to all comers and counting on the proceeds to benefit those most in need.

Jumble sales were going strong, but salvage stores were still almost unknown in Australia—St Vincent de Paul's had just two, in Sydney and Brisbane—when Lady Millie Tallis proposed running an Opportunity Shop at Melbourne's Cyclorama in 1925.

Opportunity Shop. How brilliant. Who wouldn't prefer an *opportunity* shop to one trading in *charity*, *salvage* or *thrift*, let alone *waste products*? Like William Booth, Lady Tallis had a natural flair for marketing. She and her husband, you'll recall, had just arrived home from abroad: her idea for a second-hand store to raise funds for a new wing of St Vincent's Hospital* had originated with shops she'd seen in the US and France. By one report, the opportunity shop was 'an innovation from America'. Certainly, Goodwill Stores were by then widespread in the US and perhaps, while motoring coast to coast, Lady Tallis had heard of the Opportunity Bags delivered to households by Goodwill for the collection of cast-off goods. But it seems pretty certain that her chief inspiration was *les magasins d'occasion*, the bargain shops of France. According to another report, 'Lady Tallis, when travelling on the continent, saw the public liberally patronising Opportunity Shops'—opportunity being an alternative translation of *occasion*, the French word for bargain.

Melbourne's Victoria Parade formed the northern boundary between the city proper and the crowded working-class suburbs. St Vincent's Hospital and the Cyclorama stood on the Fitzroy side of the parade. Arrangements were made with the Victorian Railways for

* St Vincent's Hospital and the Society for St Vincent de Paul are unrelated, except in both being Catholic institutions.

goods donated to the opportunity shop to be conveyed free of charge from country and suburban stations to the city's Flinders Street terminus. Well-wrapped donations could also be dropped into big wire collecting baskets at the three central railway stations. (Not literally dropped: donors were reminded that 'Teapots without spouts and cups without handles are useless.')

The opportunity shop had its opening—the Fitzroy mayoress officiating—at two in the afternoon on a Thursday in November 1925, and took £300 in its first three hours.* Said to be ideally situated to reach 'people in the congested areas', on its opening day the opportunity shop 'drew women up the hill, from north, south, east and west', all after a bargain. This was the day one lucky flapper got herself a pair of silver shoes for sixpence.

A photograph in the next morning's paper (STRANGE COLLECTION AT 'OPPORTUNITY SHOP' SALE) showed a group of genteel shoppers hovering by a wicker table at which a volunteer was writing out raffle tickets. Hard by, you could make out a wardrobe, a firescreen, a motor-bike and a bed with rolled-up mattress, against a densely jumbled background spiked with chair and table legs. In the society paper *Table Talk*, Lady Tallis and helpers—all with bobbed hair, hats and aprons—posed behind

* Call it roughly $25,000 in 2019 buying power.

a trestle table selling lamps and glassware. On shelves behind them were leant dozens of framed pictures, just one of several species of white elephants on sale.

A leading booster of the opportunity shop was the Catholic newspaper the *Advocate*—

> *Never has there been such a treasure patch in Melbourne of the relics of the might-have-been! A country store in the mining days of old never held one-half the variety of articles gathered into the capacious maw of the Opportunity Shop.*

The talk of 'treasure' was straight out of the Waste Collection Bureau's playbook. The opportunity shop could take for granted the custom of those most needy and proximate; its press coverage aimed to pique curiosity and nostalgia among the more comfortably off.

Around the curving walls of the Cyclorama were posted signs announcing the opportunity shop's various 'departments'. One that can just be made out in the press photos is GROCERIES. These were donated by households and businesses in a grand-scale Harvest Sunday-type effort—if not exactly second-hand, then second-best. Out of frame was a sign grouping MISCELLANEOUS ODDMENTS, UNCLASSIFIED, where might be found 'anything, from a gramophone record or a coal scuttle to *Sandow's Gospel of Strength*' (a body-building manual). Besides those, things sent in for sale ran to women's, men's and children's clothes, boots and shoes, ornaments, musical instruments, books, carpets, kitchen utensils, gramophones, meat safes, sofas, cots, perambulators—and geese.

Lady Tallis's opportunity shop looked like, and essentially was, 'a glorified jumble sale'. But it would trade from ten till five in the Cyclorama for nine weeks, until the end of January 1926. All that time (except for Christmas) the stock was replenished daily by deliveries brought in from the railway stations and the suburbs. The total takings were £1,800: an amount not to be sneezed at but, even so, a tiny fraction of the £60,000 raised by the fundraising appeal—all those football matches, car trials, balls and beauty contests—towards the cost of St Vincent's new X-ray and pathology wing.

The lifespan of that first opportunity shop was circumscribed by its licence: the St Vincent's appeal was permitted by the Charities Board to run only until the end of 1925, in order to give the public a couple of months' reprieve before the start of the next big fundraiser, which was for the Children's Hospital. The St Vincent's appeal organisers were publicly reprimanded for letting their opportunity shop overrun the end-of-year deadline and, in compensation, the Children's Hospital appeal was granted the use of the Cyclorama for its own opportunity shop during a couple of winter months in 1926.

Though run on broadly the same lines as the original, the Children's Hospital opportunity shop opened for just three hours each afternoon and actually sought donations of chipped crockery from cafes.

Opportunity shops seemed to catch on after that. Before 1926 was over, the Society of St Vincent de Paul opened a waste products bureau in central Melbourne, but calling it instead an opportunity shop. And soon there were op shops in Geelong, Bendigo and Adelaide as well. Some, running for only a day or two, were really jumble sales trading on the novelty of a new name. Even the pioneering Lady Tallis was prevailed upon to run her second opportunity shop—a mere stall selling trumped-up white elephants ('anything from a bat to a picture to a type writer')—at a three-day market fair staged by the Queen Victoria Hospital for Women.

A regular feature of opportunity shops, besides the name, was that they would occupy an untenanted shop rent-free or at a cut rate, giving them a main-street profile and consumer kudos.

> *The Opportunity Shop in aid of the YWCA Hostel Extension Fund was opened yesterday in the premises (kindly lent)...opposite the State Savings Bank. Good business was done during the day, when a constant stream of people purchased bargains in clothing, etc.*

Temporary shops of this sort—elongated rummage sales, rather than part of a large-scale charity salvage enterprise—had been commonplace in the US for at least twenty years, and very likely contributed to Lady Tallis's inspiration. In 'The Mother of Emily', an American short story widely syndicated in the women's pages of Australian newspapers in 1905, the titular narrator, a helper at a church rummage shop, explained the drill: 'We hired an empty store at the other end of town…It's been in progress two weeks already'—

> *You send any old things you have—anything: it doesn't make any difference what it is. And we sell them to the poor for a few cents…—many of them will buy things when they wouldn't beg for them. They get good warm clothing and stores for a song. And quite a number of us pick up odds and ends there—really!*

(It was the mother of Emily who congratulated herself on having 'enough humility herself to wear a rummage hat'.) In Australia, one of the First World War 'comforts committees'—energetic women's groups that sent socks, chocolate, writing paper and other small luxuries to soldiers—had hatched the idea of a weekly 'jumble stall' at Paddy's Markets in Sydney, with 'most gratifying results'.

But by the middle of 1927, something had solidified. The Catholic Women's League opportunity shop had been running in Adelaide's busy Gouger Street for more than a year and was bringing in enough to pay the half-yearly interest on the League's city hostel. In Melbourne, the St Vincent de Paul's opportunity shop in Melbourne lost its original central-city location after the property—on loan—was sold. It found larger premises in Flemington and settled in, offering shoppers 'anything from a button to an invalid chair' and assuring donors that 'Nothing goes to waste.'

In Britain, the salvage store movement founded there by the Salvation Army was practically dormant from the beginning of the First War to the end of the Second; charity shops were still to come. But in the US the charitable second-hand industry thrived in the decades between the wars. Both Goodwill and the Salvation Army rebranded their shops 'thrift stores', defusing connotations of salvage and welfare while still imparting a moral charge. Goodwill had emphasised quality and presentation in its stores from the start: everything cleaned, mended and sorted into departments. The Salvation Army began with depot-like stores that required customers to scramble through a mass of stuff to find what they were looking for.* But in the 1920s, following the lead of commercial retail and Goodwill, racks and bins were introduced for clothing,

* The Salvos store (or permanent 'jumble sale') I frequented in Melbourne in the 1970s still followed the original, unmediated format.

goods were clearly priced, furniture was displayed rather than treated as lumber, collectable bric-a-brac got a department of its own and, in New York City, a Salvation Army bookshop opened. By the end of the decade, for the first time, the Army's salvage enterprise earned more from its thrift stores than from paper recycling.

In her novel *The Group*, set in New York in the mid-1930s, Mary McCarthy has the bipolar Trotskyist Mr Andrews finding work in a thrift shop on Lexington Avenue whose stock was 'an instructive inventory of the passé'. (His sister had pulled some strings to secure him the job, so that she might have first dibs when good quality antique furniture came in.) Was it a Goodwill or a Salvation Army store? McCarthy doesn't say, and perhaps it was neither. Inspired by the success of those two franchises, and building on the old rummage-sale impulse, thrift stores run by local charities had been appearing on the scene in the US since the 1920s.

In Australia, the opportunity shops that followed on from Lady Tallis's seem mostly to have succumbed to the fate of all fads. Perhaps the small local charities struggled to keep up a supply of second-hand stuff; or maybe it was hard to secure rent-free premises over the long term. Or was it that, with the end of the 1920s and the coming of the Depression, *opportunity* suddenly had a hollow ring? For whatever reason, opportunity shops (by that name) were short lived in their first efflorescence.* Second-hand dealers, we know, flourished during the interwar years as fashions and technology took sharp swerves, making things redundant faster. And during the Depression years, charitable second-hand—if not actual op shops—saw something of a resurgence.

In Sydney, for instance, early in 1931 a 'wee shop' selling left-off clothing in aid of charity was set up at the Central railway station end of George Street by Lady Gordon† and a band of helpers. The venture was planned and launched without fanfare, so as not to attract the attention of second-hand dealers. Soon, though, police were needed on shop days to hold back the 'hundreds of women of the working-class' who vied to get inside. The same went for a 'dingy and cramped little shop' opened by the Brotherhood of St Laurence in Fitzroy—close by the quondam Cyclorama—in 1937, selling second-hand goods to residents of that congested district. On the day or two each month that the shop opened for business, 'police had to control the crowds pressing around'.

* Only two outfits—St Vincent de Paul's in Melbourne and the Catholic Women's League in Adelaide—seem to have kept the name 'opportunity shop'.

† Like Lady Tallis in Melbourne, Lady Gordon (née Margaret Thomas) was a former singing star turned tireless worker for charity. In aid of the comforts funds during the First War, she staged innumerable fêtes, indulged her passion for jam-making and may well have had a hand in that Paddy's Market jumble stall, precursor to the wee shop.

Such desperate popularity must attest both to extreme want and the scarcity of affordable second-hand. And to something else, too: an impulse to *shop*. Strange through it seems, the growth of consumer culture, which got such a boost in the 1920s, continued apace during the years of the Depression. Hairstyles, hem-lengths, the wireless, motor-car, refrigerator—once you bought in, there was pressure to keep up with the new, newer, newest. Good quality, hardly worn discards were now the staple of second-hand dealers' stock. When my gran bought clothes for her little girl from Mrs Nangle's second-hand stall at the Queen Victoria Market, it was with the assurance that they'd come from the best homes in Toorak, Melbourne's toniest suburb.

Mrs Nangle's prices—cheap, but not charity-cheap—would likely have been beyond the flat-out poor. The crowds that swarmed the Brotherhood shop and Lady Gordon's wee shop in George Street were doubtless driven by need—but also by the thrill of a bargain. Who could say what your hard-scrimped pennies might buy? A child's coat with a fur collar, woollen singlets for a baby, a pair of silver shoes? Whatever else, it was an opportunity to shop.

CHAPTER 10

Found

The rarest of created things is a man who always remembers his umbrella, and the train is the easiest place in which to forget it.

ARGUS (MELBOURNE), 1908

The same Gallic buoyancy that sees opportunity in a bargain turns *lost* into *found*. Paris has *le service des objets trouvés*—the Bureau of Found Objects.

'Because', as the bureau's director says, 'we do not know if they were lost or stolen. We only know that they have been found.'

In the English-speaking world, perversely, found objects are called 'lost property'. (The Japanese term, *wasuremono*, extends its definition to things forgotten.) If the Bureau of Found Objects states its business exactly, a lost property office seems to promise too much, for not all property lost will turn up there.

Whether found, lost or forgotten, most misplaced property that goes unclaimed will become, eventually, second-hand. In Paris, except for items bearing personal data—phones, laptops, keys, ID cards and documents—anything unclaimed after four months is offered to its finder (called *l'inventeur*) and, if unwanted, is sold or given to charity. The same goes in most places: after three, four, six months, items go in search of a new owner.

Unclaimed property, nowadays, is generally disposed of by tender or distributed to charities for sale in their op shops. But there was a time when a lost property auction and the apparatus supplying it ranked, for novelty, with escape artists—whose heyday also hinged the nineteenth and twentieth centuries.

The *Strand Magazine* (best remembered for the Sherlock Holmes stories) in 1895 ran an illustrated survey of London's principal lost property offices, or LPOs. Journalist William G. Fitzgerald was granted access to the Metropolitan Police LPO at Scotland Yard, as well as to those of the half-dozen railway companies whose lines converged on London. 'The great Lost Property Offices of London,' he found, 'are a truly eloquent testimony to the catholicity of forgetfulness.'

The same readers who went wild for the Holmes stories would have loved Fitzgerald's crowded account of all that he saw in the 'huge, dim-lit warehouses'. The accompanying photos, showing flash-lit recesses stacked and jumbled high and deep with teeming stuff, stirred the imagination like pictures of the freshly plundered Tutankhamen's tomb would thirty years later. 'Of course the great romance of the Lost Property Office lies in the vast numbers of strange and fearful things that find their way into this essentially human institution.' In a corner of the LPO at Liverpool Street Station, the list-loving visitor itemised:

> *a Kodak camera, a couple of violins, and a plebeian concertina; a music stand and some fishing-nets; tennis rackets [*sic*], golf clubs, cricket bats, and footballs; a bicycle and some fishing rods; a few toys, a whip, and a complete set of harness...[;] an ormolu clock and a siphon of soda-water; an ice-cream machine and a butcher-boy's tray; some tools and a coster's naphtha lamp...*

Stored together at the depot of the Midland Railway Co. was a similarly eclectic assortment—

> *a couple of barber's chairs found on the platform at Leeds, and a parrot's cage...some framed pictures, and a front-driving safety bicycle; a peripatetic knife-grinder's apparatus; a pair of crutches...a mail-cart and a trombone; a couple of hat-boxes and a lawn-mower; a gun and a Union Jack...*

There were tobacco pipes by the hundred, a set of false teeth (found in a sleeping car), seven pairs of false whiskers and piles and piles of luggage, from Gladstone bags to picnic hampers to huge Saratoga trunks.

Clothing there was in 'surprising variety': coats, of course, but also dresses, boas, fur muffs and navvies' boots. At Cannon Street station, terminus of the South-Eastern Railway, Fitzgerald was shown 'a perfect museum of tiny boots and shoes, kicked off by the fretful babies of hop-pickers' bound for the fields of Kent and Sussex. Also gleaned from the South-Eastern line were cratesful of straw hats, left and lost by seaside excursionists. Seeing a consignment of such strays brought off a train at Cannon Street, an onlooker feared there must have been an accident, 'but was assured that it was merely a weekly collection from stations down the line'. Hats of all sorts featured prominently among property turned in at any LPO: infantry and firemen's helmets, a hussar's busby, mortarboards, tall silk hats ranging in condition from 'irreproachable' to 'unspeakable'.

Unclaimed goods from freight cars and cloakrooms accounted for the more cumbersome objects in the railway LPOs. There were fewer wheelbarrows, lawnmowers and bicycles cluttering up the Scotland Yard LPO, which was stocked, mostly, with things left behind in hansom cabs, omnibuses and tramcars. Drivers and conductors of public vehicles were obliged by law to hand in found items at a police station within twenty-four hours. Anything unclaimed after a week would be forwarded to Scotland Yard. Received in 1894 were 4,948 purses and bags, 696 pairs of opera glasses, 142 watches, and, making up nearly half the total, umbrellas and walking sticks numbering 13,874.

In the railway LPOs, too, Fitzgerald had seen thickets—forests—of umbrellas, stacked in racks that reached from floor to ceiling. 'There is nothing appertaining to civilised man,' he concluded, 'that gets lost so frequently as an umbrella.' Or, if there was *one* thing that surpassed it, it was a glove: a single glove. The LPOs bagged up single gloves, a week's worth to a sack, and should anyone come seeking a missing one, the sackful would be spread out on a counter for them to scry. A photo captioned *A week's gloves (Liverpool Street LPO)* shows just such an autopsy: a rough sack spilling out hundreds of crumpled gloves, each tagged with details of its stranding.

Almost every LPO kept an adopted pet that had been left behind in its cage or carrier and never claimed. Cannon Street station had an Irish retriever named Whit; Euston had a cat and a canary. The Victorian Railways LPO in Melbourne had, for a time, a tortoise as its mascot, but it escaped into the Spencer Street railyards.

Recounting the incident, an LPO clerk expressed surprise that no one had sighted the fugitive. 'It does not occur to the officer,' remarked his listener wryly, 'that the presence of a tortoise on a railway line would not excite comment. It might easily be mistaken for a country train.'

As in the instance of seaside excursionists' hats, the character of railway flotsam would vary according to season and geography. In rural Western Australia during the 1920s, road construction advanced at a frantic pace and itinerant labourers were blamed for the profusion of property left behind on the railways. After three or four months' work, a navvy would splash out on a new working outfit of suit, singlet and boots before setting off for his next job—

> *...the change of attire often takes place in a railway carriage, and the discarded clothes are frequently left under the seat or on the rack. Another method of disposal is to leave the bundle in a railway cloak room at the small storage cost of threepence.*

Abandoned shovels, picks, mattocks and axes, all worn out, likewise marked 'the passage of the nomad'.

Even where trains were not routinely used as changing rooms, the greater portion of lost (or found) property went unclaimed.* Luggage was the item most likely to

* And that's still the case; only in Japan do restitution rates for lost-and-found exceed fifty per cent.

be reclaimed, as it tended to be labelled and identifiable by its contents. Of the remainder, the majority was presumed to be 'unhallowed by association, and unworthy the trouble of reclaiming'. Storage space being finite, once a year or oftener goods unclaimed were inventoried and put up for auction.

> *At Lost Property Store, Spencer-street Station. Unreserved Sale of salvage and unclaimed goods consisting of—Boxes of luggage, portmanteaus and content...large quantity of umbrellas and walking sticks...saddlery, fishing rods, tackle, &c., large variety of carpenters', plasterers' and painters' tools, chairs, tables, musical instruments, assortment of opera and field glasses, guns, ammunition, cutlery, brushware...&c.*

Most of those attracted by such notices would be second-hand dealers. But there were always some among the general public to whom a lost property sale was irresistible, on account of 'two of the most powerful impulses known to the human race—curiosity and the desire for a bargain'. And to the press also, the sales were catnip, always good for a paragraph or two tapping the human-interest vein.

One of the London railway LPOs estimated in 1895 that it took six weeks to assemble and sort the stock in preparation for an annual sale. The return—consistent across decades and hemispheres—averaged about £400. At a Melbourne lost property auction in 1893, a dealer offered £300 for all seven hundred lots at the outset; but the auction went ahead and realised nearly £450.

What was for sale? Ask rather: what wasn't? Milk cans, deckchairs, demijohns, mangles, bookmakers' bags, gamblers' materials, surgical instruments, typewriters, potato diggers, ladies' and gentlemen's underclothing, mackintoshes, furs, boas, sealskin bags, Masonic aprons, emu eggs, cigars, a tricycle, a trick cycle, a lady's side-saddle, ivory billiard balls, bags of cement, meat safes, accordions, violins, a bow and arrow and a statuette of Baden-Powell. That's a selection from 'the usual miscellaneous assortment of articles' offered at Victorian Railways lost property sales over the years. Among the left-behinds auctioned at Liverpool Street Station in London in 1894 were 505 deerstalker hats and 2,301 umbrellas.

Most-lost and least-claimed, four thousand-odd umbrellas were sold at Euston Station's annual sale and more than two thousand each year at the Victorian Railways auction, where ownerless umbrellas were auctioned in bundles of twelve that fetched from five to twelve shillings a bundle. At the London railway sales, they were made up in lots of between six and thirty-six, according to quality, to be hawked cheaply—but at a profit—at street corners and market stalls. Many, no doubt, were destined to be lost and found and lost again.

At a railway auction in Melbourne, walking stick sales would come a distant second and hats and caps a fair third. And behind them, 'for some strange reason, shirts'. Gloves, which figured so numerously at the London LPOs, went unmentioned in Melbourne. Are we to conclude that colonials went habitually barehanded, or was it that odd gloves were considered not worth the trouble of keeping? The two thousand single gloves sold at the Liverpool Street LPO sale in 1894 were knocked down for under £5 to a dealer who would dye them a uniform black and sell them at the London markets or direct to omnibus and cab drivers for about eightpence a pair.* That would make for a profit of more than 600 per cent, assuming a pair could be found to each glove—but I'll bet that right gloves outnumbered left, three to one.

Hats—awkward to store and stack, subject to fashion—were always a lost-property nuisance. At the auctions, they'd be sold in bulk lots to dealers, the best of them for resale, middling ones for reviving or export, and the 'unspeakable' multitude for whatever use remained. An enterprising London dealer, having bought a cheap lot of top hats at a sale in 1905, stripped off their brims,

* A far cry from a single white glove of Michael Jackson's, which would sell at auction in 2009 for US$480,000.

attached loops of string and sold them to costermongers as nosebags for their donkeys.

There would be, among the horde at any lost property sale, an eccentric coterie imbued with more than their share of curiosity and bargain-hunger. These were the bidders for travel-worn luggage, bags and boxes, sold with 'contents not specified'.* If they were empty, the fact was stated; if not, well, 'no man may know, until he has bought them what these Pandora-boxes hold'. Nor woman, either.

> *A simmer of laughter goes through the room when a lady buys a 'band-box and contents' for five shillings. 'You've been done for four-and-nine, missis,' says someone.*†

The 'contents not specified' lots—perhaps a hundred or more—guaranteed the best entertainment at any sale. Certainly, a colour-seeking journalist would find his best material there. Offered just two shillings and sixpence for a dozen 'purses and contents', an auctioneer knew to wheedle, 'Why, there may be a five-pound note in every one of them,' and the bidding would take a bound. An elderly farmer at a Victorian Railways sale forswore the

* The fascination with 'contents not specified' lives on in modern types who bid blind for the unclaimed contents of storage units (and in viewers who made the reality TV show *Storage Wars* a hit).

† They meant her purchase would turn out to be worth just threepence.

purses but bid on every swag, having once, he confided, bought one with a 'fi-pun note' sewn inside. Another bidder told of a musty old swag got for two shillings at a past sale: inside, he'd found a diamond ring and 'letters from the aristocracy'. But usually, they agreed, the most you'd find in a rolled-up swag—comfort and companion of the itinerant worker—was a pound or two of tea and sugar, a plug of tobacco, and 'a few needles stuck in a cork'.

As the auctioneer's assistant brought each 'surprise packet' forward, those watching would try to guess, from the way he handled it, at the weight of its contents. And those contents would remain a mystery until the auction ended: successful bidders had to wait till then to lift the lid, though they might hiss—in vain—to the handler, '*Is it heavy?*' Sure that he'd seen the man stagger at the effort of lifting it, the buyer of a tin hatbox—Lot 443 at a 700-lot auction—was 'simply devoured with curiosity to get it into his possession'.

CHAPTER II

Open to Offers

I have a double-barrelled gun, silver mounted and in excellent order. I want, in exchange, a double perambulator.

EXCHANGE AND MART, 1869

With the advance of consumer culture, barter—that most ancient mode of exchange—all but disappeared in the industrialised West. In the 1860s, however, barter underwent a revival through a back-page initiative of an English women's magazine.

For the cost of a penny stamp or two, readers of *The Queen* could place a notice in the magazine's Exchange and Mart column, seeking a gipsy ring or a Canadian gander, a set of fish knives or a side-saddle, and offering in exchange not money, but a cuckoo clock or an ivory fan. The wife of the magazine's proprietor, an amateur entomologist, had originated the idea with a notice seeking to swap specimens with other collectors by post.

In 1868, *Exchange and Mart* spun off into a publication of its own. Besides fossils, feathers, bird eggs, flower bulbs and poultry, advertisers sought and offered furniture, postage stamps, autographs, furs and lace, garden tools, jewellery, sporting goods, musical instruments, household appliances and more. Here's a sample from the very first issue of the standalone *Exchange and Mart*—

> *Wanted, a sewing machine in perfect order. Offered, gold locket, carved gold ring, bracelet, smelling bottle, bogwood brooch ornamented with gold leaves, two ostrich feathers, collar and cuffs of Honiton lace, silver pencil case, knapsack, castle bagatelle pachesi, an Indian game; books, music.*
>
> *I have a very handsome curly, liver-coloured retriever, which I should like to exchange for any good ornament for the drawing room.*
>
> *Photographic apparatus—A complete set for portraits; also stereoscopic camera, lens, &c. Wanted in exchange, a garden roller, engine, and barrow; but open to offers.*
>
> *I have a Bunsen's voltaic battery, with acids, copper wire, book of instructions by Lardner, and pencils*

for electric light. Want a small fernery, but open to offers.

I want a miniature billiard table, and would give a large shower bath, with force pump, and in complete order; also light double-barrel gun, by a good maker; but am open to any offers.

Pretty plainly, the items offered for exchange were regretted purchases, unwelcome gifts, enthusiasms outgrown, white elephants before their time. And how else might they be got rid of and turned to good account from the comfort of one's home in the hinterland?

The first of its kind, *Exchange and Mart* met with instant success. It began as a weekly, guaranteeing a minimum circulation of ten thousand, but it pretty soon reached many times that number of readers and was issued twice, then three times, a week. The 'Mart' section offered items for sale, but it was the 'Exchange' that drew the most attention. It was an innovation 'characteristic of the age', said a writer in the *Pall Mall Gazette*: 'a study of human nature and modern wants…in these days of a high standard of artificial needs'. Others thought that to speak in terms of *human* nature was putting it too broadly—

Acting upon [the] well-known and lamentable weakness of the female mind, some person, or persons, have hit upon a plan whereby women shall

> *be enabled to 'shop' without money...and 'bargain' without going out of doors.*

In no time, the *Exchange and Mart* was said to be practically an institution 'among ladies of the less well-to-do order of the middle classes'. The tone of the commentary hinted at there being something 'common', or misguidedly aspirational, in the *Exchange and Mart* habit. But, even caged by frugal domesticity, women couldn't help being alert to fashions and lifestyle trends.* *Exchange and Mart* gave them a degree of economic autonomy as well as the chance to develop—and change—their tastes and to take pleasure in possessions. Instead of 'Wanted', an advertisement might begin, 'I wish for...' or even 'My only wish is...'. A woman who lacked exchange-worthy material goods might put a value on her domestic expertise. One advertiser seeking a set of embroidered linen cuffs offered in exchange 'twelve highly-approved private recipes for puddings and cakes'.

Discretion was ensured, as advertisers were identified only by a number, and communications between parties to the exchange were conducted via the *Exchange and Mart* office. The genteel were thus shielded—but so were the crooks. The newspaper quickly became rife with scammers and fences unloading fake, faulty or stolen

* Though—lucky them—there was no such thing as a lifestyle then.

goods. Pranksters, too, seem to have made the most of the form—

> *Forty-eight-inch Special Challenge* [bicycle], *a magnificent machine, made to order this spring, cycle bearings, Carter's patent brake, etc., cost me £16. Would accept handsome gravestone, to be erected in Lower Norwood Cemetery, in exchange.*

At least, I hope that was a prank; otherwise it betokened a tragic change of fortune.

It had long been recognised that classified advertising sold newspapers and, in appealing to female readers, *Exchange and Mart* had tapped a new market. Untold copies were purchased each week for curiosity value alone. Of course, the paper's phenomenal success inspired imitation. An *Australian Exchange and Mart* appeared in Sydney in 1880, boasting that it could 'supply all your wants, from a baby's rattle to an elephant'. Soon there was the *Tasmanian Bazaar Exchange and Mart* and, in Melbourne, the Victorian Ladies' Work Association* ran an Exchange and Mart agency via the pages of the *Australasian*, whereby 'Private property of any description may be offered for exchange or sale,' only 'with the exception of secondhand wearing apparel.'

Even in the new century, the *Exchange and Mart*

* 'Work' here meant handiwork, not paid employment.

concept showed no signs of flagging. It made sense: as the consumer age gathered pace, people had more stuff to tire of and were beset by the lure of the novel and the new. Australia's longest-running Exchange and Mart was a column in *World's News*, a Sydney sensation rag. It kicked off during the First World War and ran until the 1950s, by which time it would traffic mainly in horoscopes, lonely hearts and sex manuals, and for sale, not exchange. But, to begin with, it wasn't so seedy—

> *If you have a bicycle you want to exchange for a camera, a gun for a banjo, a boat for a pony, or anything of that sort, from a needle to an anchor, this page offers you the best facilities in Australia.*

As that teaser suggests, in the racy *World's News*, Exchange and Mart appealed mainly to men. Here's a sample of adverts from across the 1920s—

> *Exchange young pony; sound, quiet, saddle or harness, for good photographic outfit, or good gramophone and records.*

> *Beard's Patent Bioscope [film projector], collapsible operating box, screen, limelight plant, electric arc, all fittings and spares, etc., given in exchange for a motor-cycle and sidecar, or a Ford car, or lorry.*

> *Wish to exchange bicycle, Edie coaster hub, acetylene gas lamp, and all accessories, spare tube, and*

two tins of carbide, new Major Taylor handle bars, model steam engine and boiler, complete soccer football, new bladder and pump, two books on how to make dynamos and electric motors, and how to make accumulators, 30 mixed .22 cartridges, and 100 ft comic film, for a light motor-bike.

Exchange Meccano parts, worth 45 shillings, for a concertina or accordion in good order.

*Will loan the book 'Instantaneous Personal Magnetism' for the book 'Natural Hair Culture' by Kelso Murchison, Would like also 'Paradise Lost'.**

Wouldn't we all?

In the hardscrabble 1930s, Perth's *Western Mail* introduced an Exchange and Mart column aimed squarely at 'the Man on the Land'. Practically every farm paddock, observed the *Mail*, was a graveyard of redundant equipment—

That little plough or cultivator which was replaced by a bigger one; that separator which went into the discard when your increasing herd made a larger one necessary. Somebody, somewhere would be glad

* That last advert (from 1929) was attributed not to D. Trump, but to B. Klemke of Henty, NSW. Incidentally, the jazz musician Charlie Mingus stored his pistol in a hollowed-out copy of *Instantaneous Personal Magnetism*, a self-help classic that consigned any man who played, listened to or danced to jazz 'to that hopeless class of vapid minds that are never capable of possessing magnetic values in any department of life'.

to acquire them in exchange for something useful to you.

Something like an old tractor, the same make as yours, to cannibalise for spare parts. The column ran for some years, facilitating exchanges of Model T Ford tyres for a chaffcutter, a three-ton spring trolley for three quiet milking cows in calf, a sow in pig for a saddle, plough wheels for a tanned cowhide and five tons of superphosphate 'or anything else useful' for an Indian Scout motorcycle.

The original *Exchange and Mart* would continue to be published until 2009, with a circulation of 350,000 copies a week at its pre-internet peak. Over the years, the 'Exchange' section would dwindle and the weekly would come to specialise in selling cars and other vehicles. *Exchange and Mart* lives on as a website. As for *The Queen*, since 1970 it has formed the regal half of the glossy *Harper's & Queen*. Before that, it was the style manual of the hip and happening Chelsea Set who, in the 1960s, would elevate old tatt to 'vintage'.*

* See chapter 16.

CHAPTER 12

The Antiquarian Thicket

...objects that, between the lassitude of some and the desire of others, go off to dream at the antique fair...

SURREALIST ANDRÉ BRETON, 1937

The *Exchange and Mart*—the English original—in 1926 launched an offshoot, the *Bazaar*, aimed at collectors of antiques, decorative art and curios. The twenties: that was the decade when collecting went mainstream.

A corollary of shingle-cut, jazz-licked modernity was a heightened sense of the past and its things. The widespread dissolution of country houses after the First War fed the market for old stuff, while the discovery of Tutankhamen's tomb stoked the public imagination. Nostalgia, affordability and the first stirrings of ironic kitsch-appeal* played their parts in the popularisation of collecting; so did the rise of motor car touring. And yet not everyone was a collector. After all, brand-new had never been more desired and attainable.

What makes a collector? The answers to that question undergird the modern notion of second-hand as more sought after than stigmatised. Collecting is intuitive, yearning, subjective. Magpies collect shiny things, a bowerbird likes anything blue and the viscacha, a 'gregarious' Patagonian rodent, will collect whatever it can carry off—from car keys to a loaded gun—until its warren comes to resemble a cabinet of curiosities. Ruminants have been known to achieve a similar effect by their habit of eating just about anything. The stomach of a slaughtered paddock cow might contain an 'old curiosity shop' of things ingested, including (in an instance that made news a hundred years ago) a flannel shirt, a hockey badge, hairpins, a toothpaste tube, more than two hundred nails, strands of wire and fragments of a writing slate.

But humans are not cattle. At least, not always.

To a Freudian, the collecting impulse in adulthood can be traced back to a constipated infancy. Collecting, in this view, is a means of holding things back, as a

* The word *kitsch* entered the English lexicon in 1926. At least one critic welcomed its adoption as overdue: Germans, he said, had long regarded England as 'the great country of Kitsch'.

defence against existential dread. Cultural theorist Jean Baudrillard also saw collecting ('a regression to the anal stage') as a child's way of exercising control over the world. The impulse tends to disappear, he said, at puberty and to resurface (sometimes) in men aged over forty. Collecting, in other words, equates with infantilism and impotence.

Serious scholars of collecting never fail to stress its *subjective* nature: the function of the thing collected is usually irrelevant (at least to the collector), its value relying more on sentiment than corporeal economy. A collection is bound up with the collector's identity, serving as 'an extended self', a schema for order, meaning and memory. To any collector, their collection is essentially a repository of Things + Memories—memories, often, associated with acquisition.

A 'passion for possession' seems to figure in any consideration of the genus *collector*. In Hugh Walpole's 1925 'romantic macabre', *Portrait of a Man with Red Hair*, the eponymous villain, himself a collector, characterises the type as 'not so interested in a thing when he owns it as he was wondering whether he could afford it'. One legendary Victorian collector filled thirty sheds with treasures dredged from the Thames, 'antiquities that he never looked at from one year to the next'. As William Davies King, whose collections include envelope linings of more than eight hundred different patterns, has written:

> *The collector is always waiting. Attain fulfillment and the collection ends. But fulfillment is never attained because the effect of acquisition constantly drains away in ownership, and so the hunt goes on.*

And yet the owning is not nothing. Consider the man with thirty sheds: whether or not he ever looked at their contents, he kept them, didn't he? Clearly, the passion for possession doesn't end with acquisition. It was Baudrillard who likened a collection to a harem, 'an intimacy bounded by seriality'. There's pleasure in accumulation: this *and* this *and* this...

The act of collecting, then, is (at least) as important as what is being collected.

Our particular interest here is in the active collecting of *old* stuff, in seeking rather than hoarding, and with some sense of discrimination. In his book *Collections of Nothing*, William Davies King wrote that 'Collecting is a way of linking past, present and future.' Old things—enduring, authentic things—give the collector a sense of extending their temporal reach: back before their lifetime and forward to a kind of immortality through the objects whose saviours they are. A collection of old things represents a stake in the future as well as the past. 'Just think,' mused the humorist and collector Nicolas Bentley, 'of the pleasure I shall give to some other crackpot, probably not yet born, when I pass away and all the things I've collected over the years find their way back into the junk market.'

Before the sixteenth century, pretty much the only old things collected and valued were religious relics: fragments of bones, hair, garments, even the desiccated digits of saints. The Renaissance gave birth to antiquarianism, with relics from classical antiquity as the new devotional objects, turned up (often) by ploughmen and craved by art-loving elites for their cabinets of curiosities. Interest in the *materiel* of the classical past grew with the unearthing of Pompeii and Herculaneum early in the eighteenth century, but only with the coming of the Enlightenment was culture broadly influenced by the fetish for antiquity that expressed itself as neoclassicism. Fashions, the Grand Tour, veneration of classical art and philosophy—and collecting, although 'classical' objects that looked (or were) new and accorded strictly with fashion were preferred over those bearing signs of actual antiquity.

To value an object because of its age: here was something new. Yet there was no cachet in the merely old. People steeped in a tradition of utilitarian salvage and re-use would hardly attach historical value to objects from within their cultural memory. And we have already seen how, over the course of the nineteenth century, a stigma attached itself to goods that were prosaically, usefully second-hand.

As the past—or a romantic ideal of it—was commodified by consumer culture, the antique endowed status on its acolytes. And they lavished money on it. With the exception of a few parson-antiquarians who dug up their own treasures, it was the moneyed and aspirational who were the collectors to begin with. But by the 1860s, when *Exchange and Mart* appeared, the scene was changing. The same people who'd learned to shun second-hand clothes—that is, the growing middle classes—were developing a taste for the ornamental antique.

The Victorian mantelpiece was crammed with knick-knackery. And not just the mantelpiece, but almost any domestic surface. There was even the whatnot, a spindly stand with shelves specially designed for the display of bijou ornaments. In suburban homes, many of the curios that made dusting a chore were mass-produced little trinkets, bought brand new. But there'd likely be some among them that had been picked up second-hand on a market stall, 'pretty things' in the way of old china and glass.

One measure of the difference between clutter and collecting was the matter of degree. In 1878, in the northern mill town of Bolton, a couple of old unglazed porcelain figurines caught the eye of a young grocer, who bought them for his mantelpiece. That grocer would go on to become Lord Leverhulme, the Sunlight Soap magnate, and the 'passion for possession' sparked by those humble figurines would drive him to amass an unrivalled collection of fine ceramics—20,000 pieces or more—that's now the pride of the Lady Lever Art Gallery near Liverpool.

Collecting, however modest, was a luxury. Usefulness was, by definition, not the point and an outlay on curios meant money diverted from life's staples. With increasing affluence, there was more money to spare. Only pennies and shillings perhaps, but it didn't—or needn't—cost much to become a collector. *Exchange and Mart* played its part in the popularisation of collecting, as did jumble sales and white elephant and market stalls.

Come the 1920s, with the rise of the automobile and more leisure time,* motorised tourism became a thing. And those who could afford motor-cars and daytrips into the countryside tended to have money to spend on other things, too. Tea-shops sprang up, as did shops selling old books and, especially, curios and antiques.

Who paid her calls with a sandalwood card-case?
From whose eighteen-inch waist hung that thin chatelaine?
Who smoked that meerschaum? Who won that medal?
That extraordinary vase was evolved by what brain?
Who worked in wool the convolvulus bell-pull?

* The working week, for many, was now five days instead of six.

Who smiled with those false teeth? Who wore that wig?
Who had that hair-tidy hung by her mirror?
Whose was the scent-bottle shaped like a pig?

(FROM 'CALEDONIAN MARKET' BY WILLIAM PLOMER, 1940)

In London, the Caledonian Market (formerly the city's cattle market) was the place to scour for treasures among the junk. Keen collectors would go disguised in their tattiest clothes in an attempt to bluff the dealers who still laid out their stock—a tantalising stew of the derelict and delectable—on the cobbles. American tourists and the fashionable crowd were seen as easy marks and would eventually be blamed for the ruination of the Caledonian Market. Dealers who kept shops in genteel neighbourhoods began taking out stalls at the market, displaying their prettified stock *on tables* and selling at marked prices. In the same period, the late 1920s, even provincial antique shops were said to be becoming 'ordered showrooms'. Where was the sport in that? If bargaining was half the fun ('Any price you like!' was the old familiar cry), scrounging was the larger half. Finding a diamond amid the dross—*that* was the real thrill of collecting. As Ivor Noël Hume put it: 'I find it infinitely more exciting to hunt the unrecognised and the unidentified through the antiquarian thicket than to have my prey handed to me all patched, polished and packaged, with nothing left to do but pay.'

The *Bazaar*, the jazz-age offshoot of *Exchange and Mart*, played a role in democratising the collecting of the 'old and beautiful'. Besides carrying listings of collectables for sale, the weekly paper ran articles that aimed to educate and foster fellowship among small collectors, regardless of class. The very act of collecting would elevate and ennoble the collector, whom the *Bazaar* dignified as a 'connoisseur'.

Historian Heidi Egginton believes that the popular appeal of antiques and curios in the 1920s and '30s was partly a reaction against the soullessness of the times. Religion was on the wane and urbanism on the rise, while mass consumerism promoted homogeneity and change for the sake of it. Collecting things 'old and beautiful', on the other hand, satisfied 'a deeply held need for enchantment, glamour and poetry in everyday life'. And by valorising old over new, the collector was asserting nonconformity, rejecting the easy and the ordinary in favour of self-expression. Maurice Rheims wrote in *The Strange Life of Objects* (1959) of curio-hunters: 'They are a hybrid and diverting set of people...exercising a choice that seems all the more delicate because it is sly and perverse.'

George Orwell summed up the *Bazaar*'s appeal as 'the charm of useless knowledge' and its readers as the sort who 'took pleasure in dates, lists, catalogues, concrete details, descriptions of processes, junk-shop windows'—savants and sad losers all. That accords with the 'queer sort of person' that a commentator in Sydney had supposed 'anybody who was suspected of being a collector' to be—until the surprise success, in 1933, of an exhibition in that city of antiques on loan from private collectors. All of a sudden, antiques, and collectors, were coming out of the woodwork.

Chances are, there are almost as many *varieties* of collector as there are collectors. You hear of obsessives and completists, of serendipitists and scavengers, besides the flat-out eccentrics. The choreographer Rex Reid collected porcelain hands, buying his first at the Caledonian Market in 1936 and his seventy-fourth at Melbourne's Prahran Market fourteen years later. The humorist Nicolas Bentley, in 1951, was 'perpetually on the lookout for junk' that was 'pretty to look at'. Of a bohemian bent, he hung plates on his walls, used framed pictures as placemats, and made lamps from old bottles. Junk was cheap, he said, and the more of it you accumulated, 'the less you'll notice the separate imperfections of each piece'. Philosopher Walter Benjamin assumed towards his collection of old books 'the attitude of an heir', which suggests not merely inheritance but stewardship. In New York during the 1960s and '70s Joseph Mitchell, long-time chronicler of the city's street life, used to haunt buildings under demolition, souveniring doorknobs, floor tiles, scraps of electrical wiring, nails and screws, fire-alarm boxes—all sorts of fixtures and architectural details, even bricks. These he bagged and labelled and kept as… what? *Aides-mémoire*, a personal museum, touchstones, ballast?

Ivor Noël Hume, who evolved from antiquarian to archaeologist, considered 'the commonplace of yesterday more evocative than its treasures'. Even so, writing in the 1970s, he doubted that he would ever come to appreciate the aesthetics of a plastic cup. He did concede, though, that 'As new generations of collectors grow up, so our yesterdays become their ancient history and our rubbish'—even a plastic cup—'a legacy from another age.' To the browser who sniggered at the 'monstrous detritus' for sale at the Caledonian Market, poet William Plomer had this advice—

Laugh while you can, for the time may come round
When the rubbish you treasure will lie in this place—
Your wireless set (bust), your ridiculous hats,
And the photographs of your period face.
Your best-selling novels, your 'functional' chairs,
Your primitive comforts and notions of style
Are just so much fodder for dealers in junk—
Let us hope that they'll make your grandchildren smile.

A newcomer to London, the narrator of Margaret Atwood's 1976 novel *Lady Oracle* discovers the Portobello Road market and spends hours poring over stalls selling 'the flotsam left by those receding centuries'—

> *I had never seen things like this before; here was age, waves of it, and I pawed through it, swam in it, memorised it—a jade snuffbox, an enamelled perfume bottle, piece after piece, exact and elaborate...*

To Atwood's narrator, a writer of gothic romances, the experience is like a communion: while she returns home exhausted from her Portobello Road 'orgies', back in their stalls the *things*, she imagines, 'would be glowing in the dusk, sated as fleas'.

CHAPTER 13

A Curious Trinket

Could You Tell a Treasure at a Bargain Sale?

NEWSPAPER HEADLINE, 1954

It must be apparent by now that I share with other writers on the subject of old stuff a fondness for lists, tallies, inventories, manifests and catalogues. And what is a list but a string of particularities? Here, between chapters on collectors and junkyards, let's linger for a change on the particularities: the treasure among the dross, the immovable white elephant, the curiosity that confounds then delights.

The relics from the Thames with which Thomas Layton, a Victorian antiquarian, filled his house and thirty sheds came, mainly, from mudlarks who scoured the shores and shallows for whatever they could find and sell. Their bread and butter was stuff like rope and coal and scrap metal, which went to marine-stores shops for recycling. But the mudlarks' expert eyes (and toes, since they went barefoot) met with more than just the commonplace. Coins, jewellery, even ancient relics, were turned up.*

Cast lead badges of the sort worn on the hats of mediaeval pilgrims were found with something like regularity close by London Bridge. Like the souvenir patches sewn onto parkas and rucksacks during the 1960s, these lead badges served as an ornamental record of the pilgrims' travels, as well as proof of their piety. Sold at holy sites along the pilgrimage route, each badge honoured a different saint with their emblem: say, the spiked wheel of St Catherine or the heart of St Joseph of Arimathea. As a crossing-place since earliest times, perhaps London Bridge also marked a site for ritual offerings. That's what the cluster of pilgrim's badges in the river mud seemed to suggest.

Antiquarians of the 1840s and '50s snapped them up.

---

* And are turned up still by present-day mudlarks who, far from shoeless urchins, are hobbyists like TV's *Detectorists*, with metal detectors and multi-pocket vests. Ted Sandling's *London in Fragments: A mudlark's treasures* (2016) is a tantalising account of the pursuit, past and present.

In fact, demand far outstripped supply—until 1857, when a miraculous-seeming abundance of pilgrims' badges came onto the market. The story was that they'd turned up during excavations for new docks beside the Thames; but really they'd been mass-produced by a pair of canny forgers.

A hundred years or so later, amateur archaeologists (that is to say, latter-day mudlarks) were stumped at finding relics including Bronze Age swords, Saxon brooches and Roman coins on the tidal shores of ports on the *other* side of the Atlantic. Rather than being evidence of upstart incursions into the New World, though, it seems that the relics had been dumped in the waters of American ports, along with tonnes of Thames river mud used as ballast by transatlantic vessels during the nineteenth century. In dock below London Bridge, a seagoing ship might improve its stability by having its hold filled with mud from a dredging barge—mud studded with stuff missed by the mudlarks.

The bed of Melbourne's Yarra River was paved mostly with beer bottles, according to a diver who worked for the Harbour Trust about seventy years ago. But occasionally 'mystery crates' would be found, sunk deep in the river mud, still nailed shut. They'd presumably been dropped overboard as ships were loaded or unloaded in the hectic decades after the gold rush, and went unreported—or at least, unfound. Sometimes, said the diver, they would contain valuable machinery or equipment, although he didn't elaborate as to what kind. One imagines a Victorian-era Antikythera mechanism or something in the steampunk line, but it was probably steam boilers and shoe lasts.

I can't help wondering whether there might be one extra-large 'mystery crate' still sunk in the Yarra mud. The obelisk displayed at Melbourne's 1888 Centennial International Exhibition was twenty-six metres high (or long, if recumbent on the river floor) and 135 cubic metres overall and was meant to represent all the gold—nearly 82.5 million ounces—found in Australia and New Zealand to that date. The idea was that the sheer bulk of this mammoth gold-painted column would impress exhibition visitors more than any number of zeros. At the very least, it must have stood out as a landmark at the exhibition building's entrance. 'Meet you at the golden poker': you can picture it.

This was the fourth golden obelisk, the first having been sent to London for the 1862 International Exhibition. Each was bigger than the last, of course, as more gold was added to the emulated total. But if the obelisk's accuracy was ephemeral, the thing itself was less so. When the 1888 exhibition wound up, a grand auction of fixtures was held. Lots included a derrick crane, turnstiles, flags of all nations, finger posts and umbrella stands, contents of the lost-property office, tree ferns in tubs—and the golden obelisk. Its new owner advertised in the newspapers, trying to offload it:

> *Bargain—Golden Obelisk in Exhibition Gardens, make grand look out tower, fire station, tea gardens, gentleman's villa.*

But it was still languishing at the exhibition building almost a decade later when, valued at £600, it was offered as first prize in a raffle held at a carnival there. We can only imagine how the winner must have felt.

All that glittered was not gilt, however: among the violins that gathered dust in junk shop windows the world over there was bound to be the odd Stradivarius. A Sydney man in 1944 paid two quid for a banged-up instrument made by a contemporary of the maestro and valued, once restored, at £500. That same decade, Harpo Marx paid three dollars for a junk-shop clarinet, an old French model which the bandleader Benny Goodman took a shine to. He gave Harpo a new one in exchange. Many antique wind instruments, seemingly bargains, had been dumped when the once-standard 'high', or Philharmonic, pitch was superseded in 1896.

With the advent of the diverting 'wireless' in the 1920s, the second-hand market was swamped, then as now, with obsolete home-entertainment gear: not just musical instruments but pianolas (the original jukeboxes) and even gramophones. Edna, my grandmother and a former Bright Young Thing, would recollect that the highlight of a day's jaunt on Port Phillip Bay had been skimming a whole trunkload of gramophone records one by one into the drink.* Fast forward twenty years, and gramophone records would be highly collectable—in particular, early HMVs. When His Master's Voice first adopted the dog Nipper as their trademark in 1909, they offered cash for records bearing the old label, which were then broken up, melted and re-pressed. Few of the originals survived, and Australia would come to be regarded by collectors as the last wild refuge of pre-Nipper HMVs.†

Australian archaeologists and treasure-hunters have often been surprised to find, in the rubbish pits of nineteenth-century slums or gold-rush hamlets, fragments of fine china from a much earlier date. These are thought to have belonged to heirloom pieces—that one item of

---

* According to Edna, the skimmer-in-chief was Frank Hurley, the acclaimed war photographer and Antarctic expeditioner. The discs had supposedly been sent by a record company to Antarctica, only to be spurned by over-winterers as 'no bloody good'. Hence the cry—*'NBG!'*—with which each was consigned to the bay.

† And there would be a fleeting craze, in the years just pre-TV, for home film nights with old silent-movie reels hired out by Kodak. For the full nostalgia kick, aficionados would comb junk shops for old gramophone records 'of that peculiar flavour essential to the showing of the silent film'.

cherished finery most families possessed—brought south by immigrants as a precious link with home. In the twentieth century, as that generation died out, second-hand dealers handling deceased estates would find heirloom pieces, still intact, in the humblest of settings. Amid the utilitarian furnishings of an inner-city worker's cottage there might (and did) turn up a Regency chair and a lady's dressing table pre-dating Captain Cook's landing by a hundred years.

It wasn't just the inheritors of such treasures who sometimes missed their value, but also those who acquired them to sell. In 1954 a trove of Italian cameos worth thousands of pounds came into the possession of a boy running a second-hand stall at a London market. He unloaded them for forty-five shillings, thinking he'd done well. Around the same time, a church bazaar sold for a shilling an antique footstool worth a small fortune. In 'The Hand of God', playwright Alan Bennett has a grasping antique dealer sell a framed sketch for a trifle. To her humiliation it proves to be a study by Michelangelo for the outstretched finger of God on the Sistine Chapel ceiling. And the same kind of thing still happens. Recent finds in op shops and garage sales have included: a sketch by Andy Warhol aged eleven (bought for $5); original artwork for the first *Avengers* comic ($2); an antique Chinese ceremonial cup carved from rhinoceros horn (bought for $4, sold for $75,000); and a Chinese 'Ding' bowl (bought for $3, sold for more than $2 million).

To realise the market value of such lucky finds, people usually rely on the fine-arts auction houses, Sotheby's or Christie's, which have been in the Cinderella business for a few hundred years. News of the occasional windfall is liable to trigger a tide of avaricious hope that *any* old junk might reveal itself to be treasure. In the decades between the two world wars, during which so many grand houses were shuttered and condemned, Christie's in London was inundated with stuff—skeletons, Egyptian mummies, stuffed crocodiles, instruments of torture, and much, much more—which the auction house declined to sell. But those who'd sent things in often didn't want them back, and so Christie's ended up filling a whole warehouse with white elephants. It would finally be emptied during the Blitz, courtesy of a German bomb.

The 'junk shops' which, in the first half of the twentieth century, were a favoured source of would-be treasure were mostly latter-day marine-stores shops whose trade had bent away from the recycling of cooking fat and old rope and towards the sale of bric-à-brac.* Stanley Street near the waterfront was still, in the 1930s, Brisbane's home of second-hand, perpetuating a connection with

* *Bric-à-brac* comes from the French *de bric et de broc* (by hook or by crook).

the original meanings of *marine-stores* and *junk*. The same was true in port cities the world over, particularly those that were maritime crossroads.

In the 1840s a plaster of Paris death mask, claimed to be the face of Shakespeare, was reportedly found in a junk shop in the German port of Mainz.* It had been in the collection of a German antiquarian in the 1770s, but had gone missing after his death. In the mid-nineteenth century, the mask's identification with Shakespeare was widely accepted; in fact, it was thought to have been the model for his memorial at Stratford. Then, for a long time, it was dismissed as a fake—until 1998 when new claims for its authenticity were raised and entertained.

'Nosing one day in the dust laden shelves' of a Paris junk shop before the First World War, ornithologist Gregory Mathews found, wrapped in brown paper, an eighteenth-century natural history book† so rare that this copy, now in the National Library of Australia, is the only complete one known to exist. 'It was merely a curiosity or a seventh sense that made me, mid sneezing, undo that

* The person who spotted the death mask in a junk shop and promoted its bona fides was the artist and naturalist Ludwig Becker, who emigrated to Australia in 1850, only to die eleven years later on the doomed Burke and Wills expedition.

† The snappily titled *Table des planches enlumineez d'Histoire naturelle de M. d'Aubenton, avec les denominations de M. M. de Buffon, Brisson, Edwards, Linnaeus et Latham, precede d'une notice des principaux ouvrages zoologiques enlumines*, by Pieter Boddaert (1783).

uninviting package,' wrote Mathews in his memoirs. He paid ten francs for it.

There are, to be honest, more stories of books rescued from obscurity than this or any volume could contain. But books, for the longest time, had scarcity and status built in. Like art or jewels, they were ready-made heirlooms, *meant* to be passed or sold on. In fact, even now, *second-hand* is so baked into the book's design that *second-hand book* is practically a tautology.

Junk shop, though, is a fluky term. There's no missing the inflection of General Blamey, the commander-in-chief of Australian armed forces, when, after surveying bomb damage in 1945, he declared with satisfaction, 'Japan is like a giant junk shop.' Or when a cricket writer characterised a fast bowler's performance in a crucial Test match as 'like a junk shop—all over the place'. But while some hear *junk shop* as a pejorative (as it's mostly intended), to some it's a siren's call, irresistible. For me, not even the knowledge that they routinely sold pre-loved false teeth can ruffle the romance that *junk shop* calls to mind. I love this description of a junk shop in Pitt Street, Sydney, as its new owner found it in 1946—

> *It was so full of stuff that he could scarcely get through the door...and the 'junk' literally reached to the ceilings. The dust and dirt lay inches thick over everything.*

The new man cleared out 'nearly all the original treasures' and set up as a dealer in collectable postage stamps: a trade with no tolerance at all for disorder or dust.

CHAPTER 14

Steel Salad

...you wander through long avenues of sleeping machinery of infinite variety. Huge electrical transformers jostle ship's boilers, and dead engines of war lie peacefully beside rusty ploughs.

MA DALLEY'S SCRAPYARD, 1939

Early automotive scrapyards also went by the name *junk shop*, being outgrowths of the old depots for metal and other recycling called marine-stores shops in Britain and junk shops in the US.

Before moving pictures and the gramophone, the spread of American English relied largely on newspaper wire services. Hence, well before the end of the nineteenth century, newspaper readers at distant points of the globe would have been accustomed to read of some ferrous curiosity unearthed in a US junk *shop*, when the item described was clearly of scrap*yard* dimensions. A double-barrelled cannon, for instance. The invention of a Georgia dentist during the Civil War, it simultaneously fired two balls joined by a length of chain. On its first firing the chain broke and the balls, let loose, knocked down a chimney and killed a cow. The cannon was never used in battle but would eventually wash up in a junk shop whence it was rescued to become a civic monument. More monumental still was the blockbusting prow of the *Merrimac*, the Civil War's first iron-clad warship. In 1881 it lay rusting in 'an obscure junk shop' in Baltimore—

> *This immense relic weighs 1,340 pounds, wrought iron, and as a sovereign of war and an object of interest as a revolution in naval warfare, would suit a Museum, State Institute, or some great public resort.*

But no such home seems to have presented itself.

As with the British second-hand trade, in the US the junk trade was largely relegated to immigrant workers and owners, in particular Jews, who were effectively barred from many trades. Almost a quarter of the Jews in New York were involved in the scrap trade by 1900, at which time iron was growing in demand as, for instance, iron-framed skyscrapers gave thrust to modern cities. The frames, rods, pistons, cranks, cogwheels, fireboxes and boilers that ran the steam-powered century may, when worn out, have been scrapped but they were never wasted.

Of course, it wasn't just big stuff and it wasn't just iron. As the new century began, waste-work was as fastidious and resourceful as it had been in Henry Mayhew's time fifty years earlier. In Melbourne around 1910, an enterprising widow attempting to supplement her income from a factory job bought at auction thousands of mouth organs that had been damaged in a warehouse fire. Over the course of six months, Marie Dalley and her two young daughters painstakingly extracted tiny lead staples from the instruments and sold them to a scrap dealer. Thus Ma Dalley learned the scrap-metal trade on the job and raised enough money to set up a shop selling second-hand furniture. Buying up house-lots and deceased estates, she soon discovered that what sold quickest were the old tools—things like anvils and boot-lasts—from backyard sheds. By 1915 she was salvaging her first shipwreck, raising and breaking up the vessel and selling its cargo.

The bloody First World War put old metal in high demand, and Dalley's business grew into an immense 'forest of bristling iron', for nearly forty years Melbourne's biggest scrapyard, where 'Huge electrical transformers jostle ships' boilers, and dead engines of war lie peacefully beside rusty ploughs.' As well as supplying local industry and hobbyists, she did a large export trade. The scrap business made Dalley a wealthy woman, but she was at the yard every day, ruling with 'shrewd benignity' and always in a fur coat, no matter what the weather.

Doubtless she had dealings with the likes of Jack Peacock, who combed the local tips for scrap iron, among other things. Just a couple of miles from Dalley's yard, hemmed in by train lines, docks, drainage channels and roads, an expanse of reclaimed swampland was used as a dumping ground for domestic and industrial waste. Peacock's shack and fenced-in yard—all built from scrap—formed part of the shantytown known (and deplored) as Dudley Flats. All through the Depression and into the 1940s he made a fair living, dealing in building materials culled from the neighbouring tip. With his negligible overheads, Peacock would likely have undercut Dalley on a roof-lot of corrugated iron.

Following Ma Dalley's death in 1965, her North Melbourne yard would be cleared of scrap to become the site of a kitsch faux-colonial coaching inn, incorporating historic architectural features supplied by the orgy of demolition that marked the 1960s, not just in Melbourne but in cities the world over. We saw how the writer Joseph Mitchell, in New York, would collect scrap and fixtures from condemned buildings. But while he bagged and stored them as artefacts, others used salvaged elements in their renovations and new builds. At their legendary yard in Brunswick, Melbourne's pre-eminent demolition firm,

Whelan the Wrecker, retailed a trove of stuff winnowed from the rubble of buildings they razed. As early as 1947, a building trade journal had run a feature on 'what can be done with old bits and pieces': one new home in Sydney made use of a lantern from the city's old mint, a carved unicorn and lion from its first courthouse, and the stone of three convict-built cottages sunk into a swimming pool. Seventy years later, when a row of Victorian-era terrace houses was demolished to make way for a new Sydney motorway, salvaged features—fireplaces, cast-iron lacework, verandah tiles, doors, chimney pots, and more—would be offered for free to displaced house-holders for their new homes.

But wait. On the subject of scrap, we need to turn back to the start of the twentieth century, when motor-cars were revving their engines. In fact, we might look back twenty or thirty years further, to when the internal-combustion engine was being tinkered into existence. Where do you suppose its inventors got the parts to tinker *with*? Junk shops and marine-stores yards yielded lengths of pipe, machinery parts, and all the odds and ends that would eventually add up to a working model.*

* The same went for the first TV transmitter and receiver, made from bicycle parts, cocoa tins, lantern glass, sealing wax and string. Just think: the key technological and cultural influences of the twentieth century—like those of every century before it—originated from second-hand materials.

Their sights firmly fixed on a future of new vehicles, early auto manufacturers including the assembly-line pioneer Henry Ford failed to anticipate a market for second-hand cars. By the 1920s, there would be one car to every three households in the US and the industry was coming to realise that, to sell new cars, they'd have to accept trade-ins. But trade-ins increased the availability of used cars, which undermined the sale of new. So serious was the threat to their business model that manufacturers proposed the mandatory destruction and recycling of second-hand cars. Ford went so far as to establish a *dis*-assembly line. (It proved unprofitable.)

Sales of second-hand cars would soon, and forever, far outstrip the sale of new.* But not every old car was traded-in or sold in working order. Already, in the 1920s, as many as a million cars were 'retired' each year in the US. Auto wreckers were glad to have them. Cars would be broken up, the steel bodies mostly sent for recycling and the parts stripped out and sold as spares. There are even accounts of car parts—the long cross-members, steering columns and axles—being used by the construction industry as concrete reinforcement.

The old name of *junk shop* (or, increasingly, junk *yard*)

* A development that economist Bernard Jullien applauds as a stumble in the march of capitalism. His essay on the subject is titled 'The Second-hand Car Market as a Form of Resistance'.

would cling, affectionately, to the wrecker's yard for a generation or more. And not just in the US; in Australia, too, junk shops were talked about as temples of automotive reincarnation.* In 1934, 'in the corner of a junk shop', a West Australian youth spotted the disarticulated remains of an old motorbike. There was only one wheel, so he selected another from a pile, paid ten shillings and took the lot home in a crate to his father's garage. 'When assembled the parts became a 5/6 pocket valve Indian of 1914 make, a relic of the earliest twin-cylindered American machines seen in this State.' Score! And it clocked nearly sixty miles per hour in the local car club's speed trials.

Stories like that must be as mouth-watering to a habitué of swap meets as the thought of a flapper's silver shoes is to me. But 'vintage', at that time, was an idea without a name. 'There is no sentiment in the heart of the wrecker,' declared a nameless feature writer in 1927, even though 'he deals in the wares which make sentiment possible.'

> *Mudguards hang from the ceiling; radiator shells depend from odd nails; wheels of all sizes are stacked in tiers and protrude in sudden curves from gigantic heaps of old batteries, seats, engine blocks,*

* Doubtless journalese was partly responsible for the offshore adoption of *junk shop* and *junk yard*, but the terms also signified the Americanness of the automobile age.

> *crank-shafts, blackened pistons, steering columns, and rubber-bare tyres. Carefully stowed away in tracks are the parts most often demanded—crown wheels, pinions, gear sets, steering boxes, stub axles, springs, torque rods. A steel salad…*

If the wrecker was no sentimentalist, the writer certainly was. To the mounds of dismembered parts lying about the yard, he was moved to supply an epitaph: 'Scattered and maimed and rusted they lie, that had each its part in a grand song of speed.'

Mostly, though, the wrecker's yard was where a driver went, out of necessity rather than sentiment, for spares to keep their old model on the road. Old, banged-up models would be seen more often on country roads, 'where appearance is discounted and utility is the thing', than in cities. A car that ended its days in a rural district was as likely to be put out to pasture as sent to a junk yard, 'driven into the home paddock for the last time and left to rot'. Then, 'When he wants to repair the roof of the shed, or build a new fowlhouse, the owner will ruminatively grasp a sledge hammer [and] smash off a useful portion.'

The scrap trade grew in tandem with the auto industry, so that, by 1950, there were an estimated twenty-five thousand auto scrapyards in the US. Steel was in strong demand, and wreckers streamlined the salvage process by burning cars in pit incinerators, eliminating everything but the metal—and making no small contribution to America's air pollution. In the mid-1950s, increasing labour costs made it less viable for steel mills to process out the small amount of copper in the steel of car bodies. As demand for auto salvage fell off, scrapyards closed down and old cars became a burden. Between 1955 and 1970, countless millions* of vehicles were abandoned: in the wild, in the water, on backroads, highways and city streets. In 1969 alone, seventy thousand cars and trucks were abandoned on the streets of New York City. As President Nixon told Congress the following year, 'Few of America's eyesores are so unsightly as its millions of junked automobiles.' Not only were they an eyesore, but leaking fluids and leaching metals were causing massive pollution to soil and waterways.

Just coming into use were gargantuan metal shredders, capable of efficiently reducing cars to their constituent parts for recycling. A campaign commenced to round up all the hulks and put them through the shredders; but not until China's demand for steel peaked, in 2008, would the very last of the rust-buckets be hauled out of the woods.† (Not out of the barns, though, or not entirely.

* Between nine and forty million was one best estimate.

† Adam Minter's 2013 book, *Junkyard Planet*, conveys the drama and minutiae of the scrap metal trade. For example: 'The average American car is shredded with $1.65 of change inside.'

'Barn finds', garaged or put up on blocks decades ago, still occasionally turn up—like a 1952 Type 1 Volkswagen Beetle that went to auction in 2017. It had been found in a barn, with just a little body rust, 77,000 miles on the clock, and the original owner's wooden skis still strapped on the back.)

Sales of cars in America today stand at something like five second-hand for every two sold new. In much of Africa, the ratio of new to used is between 1:10 and 1:20, with vehicles on the road on average twice as old as in the West. Because Antwerp has long been the port of lading for Europe's used-car exports to West Africa, in Nigeria second-hand vehicles are referred to as 'Belgium'. The same label extends to cars imported from elsewhere, including the preferred American models. To prolong their life on the road, sprawling outdoor markets, or auto-mechanic villages, sell and fit 'Belgium' spare parts. Lagos Island was Nigeria's original auto spare parts mecca, but dealers were driven off in the 1990s as the island underwent upscale development. Now their headquarters is the Super International Market on the Lagos outskirts, the biggest market of its kind in Africa, where hundreds of dealers sell parts, dismantle vehicles, and make on-the-spot repairs. Away from the markets, roadside mechanics ply their trade all through Nigeria, with salvaged spare parts and the know-how to keep almost any rattletrap running.

CHAPTER 15

Mending vs Ending

The good citizen does not repair the old; he buys anew. The shoes that crack are to be thrown away. Don't patch them. When the car gets crotchety, haul it to the town's dump.

HOUSE & GARDEN MAGAZINE (US), 1930

Old-time salvage made a comeback during the two world wars. At home, at the front and at points between, not a thing escaped scrutiny as potentially useful or otherwise valuable.

In Paris during the First World War, the British army had a vast salvage depot served by a railway siding, into which would roll 'wagon-loads of soiled, bloodstained, and tattered uniforms'. At the depot, hundreds of French civilians, most of them women, were employed in sorting, cleaning, disinfecting and repairing the uniforms, sending as many as possible back to the muck-sodden soldiers at the front.* Uniforms arriving at the depot so bloodstained or shredded as to be past repair were shipped off as rags to the shoddy mills still running at Dewsbury, near Leeds. The rest would be returned to a condition 'almost as good as new'. Besides garments of wool and cotton, the salvage workers had to revive coats lined with fur or sheepskin, leather jerkins and the long rubber boots worn in the trenches. Of the latter, two thousand pairs were washed and dried daily; any that were too far gone were used to patch the rest. Many of the female salvage-workers adopted as their work-gear old British army jackets, complete with stripes denoting rank.

Caught short when the war began, the British army had had to call, at first, on stocks of second-hand military clothing. In the trade, old uniforms were generally considered an unprofitable line; but not in this instance. One dealer who was later charged with profiteering was in possession of thirty thousand second-hand army overcoats when war broke out. He sold them back to the army at a little over three times what he'd paid for them. At Tobruk in 1941, Australian troops would be issued with

* By contrast, Union Army officers in the American Civil War received orders that 'cast-off clothing of our soldiers'—those killed in battle, mainly—was to be collected and burnt. Otherwise, Union uniforms might offer relief to 'the rebels', who were desperately short of clothing—or might even provide cover for spies.

corduroy shorts cut down from light-horsemen's jodhpurs that had been in mothballs since the last war.

During World War II, the Australian Army Salvage Corps operated with, well, military precision. Whenever a new uniform was issued, an orderly from the Salvage Corps would be on hand to retrieve the one cast off. Clothing was repaired, cleaned, fumigated and reissued—but not to the fighting forces. Instead, dyed a distinctive shade of burgundy, it became the uniform of prisoners of war and internees in Australian detention. The Salvage Corps' central depot had itself been salvaged, being built on reclaimed swampland and some of its buildings constructed from packing cases in which Fairey Battle bombers were shipped, in parts, from Britain.

Léon Werth was among the millions who fled Paris and the advancing German army in May and June 1940, to seek shelter in the countryside. Quartered in villages and farmsteads with other novice refugees, Werth 'heard the word *salvage* used in a new sense that seemed strange to me'—

> *everyone who brought back things found on the road (whether it was a motorcycle or a handkerchief) or looted from abandoned cars said candidly, 'Here's what I salvaged…'*

The roads, the paths, the fields, all were strewn

with apparently ownerless property. Finding themselves overburdened, those fleeing would shed their prized possessions along the way. Houses left unoccupied in the exodus were looted by soldiers, the contents of drawers and cupboards emptied on the floor and anything not carried off—'from the can of preserves to the typewriter'—left scattered, just waiting to be 'salvaged'. Yet, said Werth, 'Indignation would be hypocritical here.' Serving in the last war, he'd seen plundered French farms in places through which only French soldiers had passed. 'This form of looting is an act of soldiers, not only Germans,' he wrote.

Valuables such as wristwatches and fountain pens, looted from dead Allied troops, were on open sale in Singapore at the end of the war. 'A watch I saw displayed in a shop in Bras Basah Road to-day,' noted one Australian journalist, 'was inscribed: "To Reg, love from Mother, January 1940."' Australian prisoners of war had been known to sacrifice their own valuables—love letters, diaries, even banknotes—for use as cigarette papers. One soldier ended up smoking the handwritten account he'd composed, eight pages long, of his escape from Singapore.

In the *Bazaar*, at the end of the 1920s, a dealer in Brussels had advertised—

> *Relics of the Great War for Sale. Canada and English military badges, also drums with paintings and crest of regiment…*

Even—or especially—with lived memories of the First World War still vivid, military paraphernalia gleaned from the fields of Flanders counted as collectable. (Similarly James Boswell, passing through the Scottish highlands *en route* to the Hebrides in 1773, eighty years after the Glencoe massacre, observed that battle shields had been turned to civilian use as lids for milk barrels.)

With shortages on the home front during the world wars, military salvage not needed for the war effort often went to clothe and provision those in state care. 'The shoes once worn by a WAAF may now be worn by an inmate of an Old Women's Home, and a military boot may give good wear to a lunatic pottering about the vegetable plots at Claremont Asylum in Western Australia. Superannuated uniforms were also sent to orphanages, on the proviso that 'buttons and badges should be removed, and that all material of a distinctly military character must be dyed and printed on the inside with the name of the institution'. On top of all that, of course, the clothing would have had to be cut down to size. And remember those corduroy jodhpurs? When they were refashioned as army shorts, the redundant knee pads went to make slippers for hospital patients.

In the years after World War II, ex-military stock flooded onto the market as 'army surplus'. Not just clothing, but things like toothbrushes, sold by the thousand as typewriter cleaners. Also available dirt cheap was no end of mechanical stuff—valves, lenses, switches, you name it—at least some of which went into making quack medical devices. Certainly, the US Food and Drug Administration blamed war surplus for the creation of such 'worthless machines' as the Portable Desert Air Maker and a gadget with flashing lights and electrodes that was claimed to be 'a sure thing for cancer, hardening of the arteries, abscess of the liver, and deafness'.

Army surplus stores made for a new feature in the second-hand landscape and one that, surprisingly, would outlive the era of post-war austerity. Goods that, in the past, dealers would have dumped in offshore markets seemed finally to have shed their stigma. Army surplus would come to be widely appreciated on the peacetime home front as cheap, practical and durable—and even, eventually, as modish.

But in wartime, salvage was a two-way street. Across the martial sweep of history, ploughshares must have been beaten *into* swords as often as the proverbial obverse. Foreign diplomats besieged in Beijing during the Boxer Rebellion of 1900 relied for their defence on improvised weaponry: a fire extinguisher was remodelled as a gun, with bullets cast from candlesticks and ashtrays. And at the dissolution of the monasteries under Henry VIII, abbey bells were melted down for ordnance.

So it went during the world wars—but on an industrial scale. Organisations such as the Red Cross mobilised the flow of recyclable goods and materials to the war effort. Some of the stuff collected was usable by the military, some was sold to industry with the proceeds put towards war work: first-aid supplies, 'comforts' for soldiers, support for their families. In 1917, a Red Cross 'junk shop'—actually a collection depot—put out a call for medicine and pickle bottles, rubber tyres and treacle and tobacco tins.

Metal scrap of all sorts was of enhanced value in wartime. During World War II, this value was made explicit in public appeals, or scrap drives: 'An old bucket will make three bayonets...One flatiron equals 2 steel helmets or 30 hand grenades.' Affluent American households were asked to sacrifice their washing machines to make incendiary bombs, lawnmowers for artillery shells, and even golf clubs on the assurance of their being transformed into machine guns. Aluminium cookware and toothpaste tubes were in high demand for bomb-making—for which purpose a surviving section of the German zeppelin *Hindenburg*'s lightweight frame was (with no small satisfaction) also sent to be melted down.

Farming communities cleared their sheds and paddocks of scrap iron, 'for patriotic purposes', there being, in the wheat belt of Western Australia as elsewhere, 'hardly a farm which has not a supply of old plough shares, etc.' The accumulated stock of a Red Cross salvage depot at Broken Hill in 1941 echoed that of a marine-stores dealer a century earlier—

> *One room...is devoted to a heterogeneous mass of old clothes, and the back yard is a valuable depot of bottles, bones, bedsteads, tins, wires, the torso of an old T-model Ford, and almost every other kind of rubbish you can imagine.*

Paper of all sorts was collected and sold back to the paper mills, likewise rags to the flock mills. Melbourne's Red Cross waste products depot—'the father and mother of all junk shops'—employed, at its wartime peak, more than five hundred volunteers daily. In charge was none other than Ma Dalley, the scrapyard queen.

Women were vital to salvage operations on the home front, not just because men were away at war but as managers of the domestic realm. 'This is a woman's job,' declared the American Fat Salvage Committee, in its campaign to promote the hoarding of cooking fat to be used in making nitroglycerine for anti-tank munitions. Female 'Salvage Commandos' went door to door in some US cities, spreading the word about the patriotic uses to which aluminium hair curlers and worn silk stockings could be put. (Stocking silk was ideal for bagging the gunpowder charges that fired artillery shells.)

Wartime shortages led to strict government regulations, dictating how much (or really, how little) fabric could be used to make any item of clothing. Flared skirts, double-breasted suits, and trousers with cuffs were among the styles outlawed in what amounted to a war on fashion. Women in particular were assured that, for the duration, 'their present wardrobes will not be made obsolete by radical fashion changes'. In both Britain and Australia new clothing was rationed; each person or family was issued a limited number of coupons to buy specified items. Second-hand clothing, however, was exempt from rationing and that market accordingly flourished, as did the informal trade in hand-me-downs. There was also a 'coupon racket' whereby wealthy women whose style was cramped by rationing would offer their servants 'big supplies' of cast-off clothing in exchange for coupons.

With most people wearing out their old clothes rather than replacing them, and with cash of limited value to a population who could buy only as much as their coupons allowed, second-hand dealers and rag merchants were forced to offer enticements. Where ol' clo' men in Mayhew's time had given crockery and ornamental glass in exchange for cast-offs, their twentieth-century counterparts offered goldfish as inducements and even, as shortages continued into the 1950s, new-fangled ballpoint pens. Costume designers on British wartime films struggled to dress their stars, having to improvise outfits from old curtains (à la Scarlett O'Hara), tablecloths and even pram covers.

The Australian radio serial 'Dad and Dave' in 1942 presented a comic take on the clothing shortage. 'No community anywhere has proved itself keener in supporting the war effort than Snake Gully,' ran the promo for an episode in which Dad and Dave set about 'converting some of their about-to-be-discarded clothes into garments which can still be worn'. Their efforts, listeners were assured, 'are not without their funny side'. People's actual experience offered fewer laughs, if letters to the women's pages are any guide. There were families who suffered real deprivation as they struggled to keep themselves decently clad. Those living in country districts, without a ready source of second-hand, had it hardest. And people generally who, over a generation or more, had learned to associate cast-offs with shame felt the sting of it—for all that the situation was shared.

Still there was a kind of valour in 'making do'. A reader of the *Australian Women's Weekly* in 1942 proudly sent in a photo of her son and daughter dressed in outfits she'd made from railway uniforms belonging to her husband, who had joined up. 'In making the tunic I used two pairs of trousers.' Wartime thrift—whether in eking out clothes or hoarding kitchen fat—was an act of patriotism.

Newspaper editorialists at the turn of the century had praised the 'real, level-headed, practical philanthropy' of 'thrifty housewives' who parted with surplus household goods to benefit the Red Cross. 'Houses are likely to be swept and garnished wholesale for the soldiers of the Queen,' then fighting in the Transvaal. Two wars later, government slogans like 'Use it Up, Wear it Out, Mend It, and Make Do' would still extol thrift. Or rather: not *still* but *again*.

The mend and make do culture on the home front during and after World War II was a throwback to an ethic that had been losing ground since before the First War. In pre-industrial times, a limited supply of stuff meant that everyone practised thrift, out of necessity. For most, new wasn't an option: cast-offs and leftovers were all there was. And until there were *products* to solve problems, people either made or made do.

At Paddy's Markets in Sydney in 1905, old socks were sold at a dozen pairs for a shilling—

> *The thrifty mother undoes a bundle of them and examines the feet. A few small holes are all that she discovers. A couple of cards of cotton, and an afternoon's work, and she'll have good stockings for a twelve-month.*

Calico sacks that came into the home filled with flour, sugar or stock feed might, once empty, find long use as aprons, tea towels, pillow cases, nappies or sanitary napkins, or be sewn together into bed sheets or underwear. There'd be prizes offered at country shows for 'the best parcel of children's clothing made from left-off clothes'.

But 'domestic science', concerned with rationality and, especially, with hygiene, was beginning to replace old notions of thrift with new. A 1913 home economics textbook advised housewives-in-training not to 'spend too much time on old garments'. Mended silk, in particular, inevitably gave the appearance of 'premeditated poverty'—a waste of both time and reputation. It would be a lesser waste to discard the garment.

Increasingly, the mending and re-use of one's own old things came to be tinged with poverty and shame, bordering on the stigma of second-hand. The shirking of traditional stewardship was legitimised by jumble sales, thrift stores and, for the wealthy, dealers in discarded finery, all of which enabled people to dispose of things without having to declare them worthless. As moving pictures, motor cars, pictorial newspapers and then wireless amped up the culture of consumption, *thrift* came to denote not *making do* but, rather, spending money wisely. When makers-do laid aside their workbaskets, took up their purses and sought solutions in the marketplace—no Paddy's Market this, but a hall of mirrors—they were entering a world of stuff without end.

ᔕ

From 1908, Ford produced its Model T virtually unchanged for nearly twenty years. Over that period, thanks to assembly-line efficiencies and economies of scale, the price of a Model T fell from $950 to less than $300. What made Henry Ford resistant to the idea of Ford dealers accepting and selling trade-ins wasn't just that he wanted to sell more *new* cars but his insistence that the Model T was 'so strong and so well made that no one ought ever have to buy a second one'. Ford was stuck in the kind of steam-age thinking that valorised sturdiness and long life in machines. The-car-as-fashion took him by surprise (though goodness knows, gigs and carriages had always been subject to trends). By 1923, General Motors had sniffed the breeze and began introducing a new model each year. The difference between one year's model and the next generally had more to do with styling than what was under the bonnet—although there were technological tweaks and refinements that purported to, and sometimes really did, make the new model superior to the old. Either way consumers bought it, trading in and trading up. Eventually, Ford had no choice but to diversify, starting in 1927 with the Model A.

It may have been radios that did the most to create a mass market based on technological, as well as stylistic, obsolescence. New models of radio appeared constantly, not just annually, during the twenties. As with cars, they became more affordable and that too fed into the craving to upgrade—to a bigger unit, say, or one with more knobs—or to sport the latest look. Soon, refrigerators would follow suit. Really though, this consumer revolution all followed from industry's realisation that if people would cast off *a car* that still ran just fine, then what *couldn't* they be led to think of as disposable? At back of it—and in front of it, too—was the lure of the new. Novelty, it seemed, was irresistible.

The dark art of consumer marketing hit its stride during the 1920s and '30s, popularising the notion of accelerated obsolescence as a measure of progress, a release 'from the shackles of tradition, from outworn equipment and ideas'. Even the Depression did relatively little to slacken the consumerist rhetoric. Commentators often invoked *machines* and *the machine age*, and urged the need to keep the machines going. In 1930, readers of *House and Garden* were told, 'The good citizen does not repair the old; he buys anew.' Because, of course, 'Wearing things out does not produce prosperity,' as one advertising man explained in 1932, 'but buying things does.' That same year, in Aldous Huxley's dystopian *Brave New World*, infants were indoctrinated with murmured earworms—'Old clothes are beastly', 'Ending is better than mending'—because, as the Controller decreed, 'We don't want people to be attracted by old things. We want them to like the new ones.' Who was echoing whom here?

Even as consumers were taught to disdain old things, though, one of the chief side effects of accelerated obsolescence was a flood of second- (and third- and fourth-) hand goods. A regime of regular replacement by the comfortably-off put their discarded cars and radios within reach of those less so. Now even the poor could aspire to non-necessities. It was during the 1920s that charities like the Salvation Army and Goodwill, keen to dilute the taint of cast-offs and welfare, rebranded their salvage outlets as thrift stores. They understood that the lower classes could now own last year's model rather than goods that were all but worn out, and might be inducted to the status of consumers: raised out of want; made to want more.

In the fifteen years after World War II and its lagging privations, consumer spending leapt ahead as never before, spurred on by marketers who were perfecting the art of the pitch. At the forefront was the fashion industry. As a Manhattan rally of clothing retailers was exhorted in 1950, 'Basic utility cannot be the foundation of a prosperous apparel industry. We must accelerate obsolescence.'

Or, as the semiotician Roland Barthes would put it thirty years later: 'The more the rhythm of purchase exceeds the rhythm of dilapidation, the stronger the submission to Fashion.'

The consumer ethic, perfected, is concerned less with need or use than with pleasure. An impulse—pleasure through purchasing power, new for the sake of novelty—that was once the exclusive realm of prestige has now reached democratic saturation.

But remember, newness is relative. In the passage from Shakespeare's *The Tempest* that inspired Huxley's title, Miranda's exclamation of delight—*O brave new world, That has such people in 't!*—draws from her father the wry response: *'Tis new to thee.*

What makes a thing *new* is the old thing left behind.

CHAPTER 16

What Did You Wear in 1969, Grandmama?

'My child, that was the year when fashion was born in the junk shops, the flea markets, the Army surplus stores.'

PRE-EMPTIVE NOSTALGIA IN THE *AUSTRALIAN WOMEN'S WEEKLY*, 1969

A sprawling second-hand shop opened in an old toy factory on Brunswick Street in Melbourne's Fitzroy in 1965. Run by the Brotherhood of St Laurence, the shop specialised in furniture, books and 'theatrical' items, all 'artistically arranged' by the manageress, Mrs R. Jones.* 'The theatre section,' it was envisaged, 'would be a happy hunting ground for anyone who has ever enjoyed fancy dress occasions'—

* Mrs Jones was the mother of TV quiz champion and future Labor politician Barry Jones.

> *There's everything you can imagine, from Scots bonnets to Spanish shawls and bridal gowns. You can buy tinselled blouses for 7 shillings, and handsome capes for £3, feather boas from £1, ostrich feathers for 6 shillings, military style uniforms for £2, and striped blazers for 15 shillings.*

The stock, from the sound of it, must have come from the back of wardrobes undisturbed from the 1920s or earlier until their owners' recent decease. The boas, blazers and boaters—useless as everyday wearables but not yet antique—were the kind of sartorial white elephants that could be hard to shift in opportunity shops and jumble sales of the period. Pretty soon, though, buyers were flocking to the Brunswick Street store. 'Mrs Jones says that there has been a terrific demand from "young blades" for bowler hats, and many lasses have come in to buy Charleston frocks for party wear.'* And not just for fancy dress; there was demand from schools for end-of-year concerts and amateur theatre companies with entire casts to outfit.

In Australia, op shops hadn't progressed far since before World War II. In some places, city and country, organisations that had collected materials for salvage during the war carried on in the op shop line, recycling goods in a

* Fancy dress, if my parents' efforts were anything to go by, was a far more elaborate and wholehearted undertaking among ordinary suburbanites then than it is nowadays.

small way, locally: an op shop run by the Glen Innes Rotary Club was originally the Patriot Shop. No boots or shoes and only 'slightly used' clothing that had been dry-cleaned was accepted for sale at Bowral's Bong Bong Street op shop. Lorne's hospital op shop was, like many, itinerant for a time, operating rent-free out of vacant shops until it secured a permanent home. In Melbourne, the Brotherhood of St Laurence had a growing handful of shops, the retail face of its long-running charitable salvage operation; and the matronly suburb of Camberwell had the Voluntary Helpers' Shop, raising money to house the aged and doing its bit to make second-hand respectable. A Sydney op shop in support of the Peter Pan Kindergarten claimed an 'equal share of the glamour' offered by its neighbours—couture salons, espresso bars—in cosmopolitan Rowe Street. Headlining second-hand stock from 'famous overseas fashion houses', catwalk parades in the shop's front window drew lunchtime crowds and top-shelf buyers.

In England, Oxfam had launched its first shop in 1947, when a public appeal following the Greek civil war left a surplus of donated clothes and bedding. And in the US, which led the world in consumer spending and shedding old for new, thrift shops were a steady presence, an undercurrent to the middle-class mainstream.

But there was a cross-current rising: in retrospective

shorthand, call it 'youth culture'. A strain of rebellion, stirred by rock and roll and commodified by TV, began, from the mid-1950s, to glamorise the offbeat and taboo. And what better (and cheaper) way to mortify the squares than by dressing ostentatiously in second-hand?

American colleges, in 1957, were swept by a fad for old raccoon coats. The 'coon coat was an essential Jazz Age accessory, but the craze had been dead thirty years until it was revived by two young Greenwich Village bohemians, Sue Salzman and her husband Stanley. After Sue found a raccoon fur in a junk shop ('She was on a real twenties kick—blue-black lipstick and her raccoon coat') all her friends wanted one. In a warehouse, she discovered bales of the coats which she bought for next to nothing. They were leftovers from another craze, a few years earlier, which had seen old raccoon coats cut up for Davy Crockett hats.

Sue and Stanley ('a good-looking fellow clad in a fashionably ancient T-shirt') would source and sell close to 1,500 old raccoon coats. After one was modelled in *Glamour* magazine, the college-wear supplier Lord and Taylor's offered to buy all that the Salzmans could find, but as Stanley told the *New Yorker*—

> *we go to the dealers, and they give us the old story: most of the raccoon coats they had were cut up for those damn hats. Before the Crockett boom, there*

> *was believed to be a supply of about two million old raccoon coats in the country...We could sell fifty thousand coats right now, if we could locate them.*

Some furriers, failing to register 'the shock value in the battered majesty of a thirty-year-old raccoon coat', supposed that a *new* coat would do just as well. Lord and Taylor's got it, though, advertising 'vintage raccoon coats, in a state of magnificent disrepair' at $25 apiece.

The term 'vintage', applied to clothing, was something new. It had first been tried out ten years earlier, as a garnish to pre-worn *haute couture* auctioned at swank New York fundraisers. But the label wouldn't catch on until the late 1970s. For now, a certain *seediness* ('battered majesty', 'magnificent disrepair') was key to the countercultural appeal of gear that was not merely second-hand, but old. That it was, preferably, older than its wearer left it untainted by fashions that had lapsed within their lifetime, making it less a revival than a disinterment. And besides a ghoulish glamour, there was sartorial irony at play when beatniks wore their parents' courting clothes. The plumage bespoke an attitude.

Eight years later in Melbourne, the theatre department of the Brotherhood shop in Brunswick Street was, had Mrs Jones only known it, poised to catch the attitude-as-fashion wave. After Mick Jagger appeared on British TV in 1966 wearing a red Grenadier guardsman's jacket, fancy dress would become streetwear. The Beatles, Jimi Hendrix, Eric Clapton—all would parade Victorian military tunics, boating blazers and comical hats of the kind that Mrs Jones had in plenty. The press would brand this outbreak of ironic dandyism 'the peacock revolution'.

That revolution had originated a few years earlier in the rarefied reaches of King's Road in London's Chelsea. In reaction to the Mod styles popular with the working classes, a bunch of young aristocratic types fetishised into fashion the faded grandeur of their families' former status. They adapted Victorian and Edwardian styles in a kind of twisted nostalgia* that combined reverence and ruin. Jagger would buy his guardsman's jacket from a King's Road boutique the name of which—I Was Lord Kitchener's Valet—captured the vibe to perfection.†

I Was Lord Kitchener's Valet had begun as a market stall in Portobello Road before joining the scene on King's Road, alongside Granny Takes a Trip, Past Caring and Antiquarius. As well as antique military gear unearthed in army surplus stores, they sold, at premium prices, such treasures as beaded flappers' dresses, gangster-style suits,

* But then, when is nostalgia *not* twisted?

† It helps (though not much) to know that Lord Kitchener was Britain's war minister during World War I. His was the face and pointing finger that featured on recruiting posters with the doom-filled words, 'Your Country Needs YOU.'

fringed shawls and ruffled Victorian undergarments. Celebrities shopped there and the modistes and their muses, who'd pioneered the look and embodied it, themselves became fashion icons. Among them were Patti Boyd, who married a Beatle* and Australian model Janni Goss.

'It is the big thing to wear old clothes,' Goss told the *Australian Women's Weekly* in 1966. 'I started collecting in Melbourne from the Opportunity Shops, and when I came to London I was called the smartest girl in town.' The key to bringing old styles up to date, she confided, was just to 'chop 20 inches or so off the hemline'.

Designer Jenny Kee arrived in London from Sydney in 1966, aged nineteen, and made a beeline for King's Road. Working as a sales assistant at the Chelsea antique market, she was supplied with 'lots of antique clobber to wear', making her a walking advertisement.

The hunt was on for seriously old clothes. London department stores plundered their storerooms, turning up stashes of unsold stock. Tailors and gents' outfitters, who'd long accepted old suits in part-payment for new, likewise had their backrooms cleared out. Attics were ransacked and, in country houses, rooms unopened for decades revealed troves of musty garments fit for a rock

* George.

star. Stockpiled theatrical wardrobes, even early costumes from the Ballets Russes, were brought to light. If they were a trifle seedy and moth-nibbled, so much the better.

Among hippies and their imitators, especially, precious old clothes were treated in a spirit more of ruin than reverence. After all, frayed hems and cuffs signalled authenticity *and* the debasement of capitalist values. Speaking of which, it wouldn't take long for mainstream fashion to appropriate the counterculture's look: tailored waistcoats, collarless 'granddad' shirts, floaty fabrics and lacy trim, maxi skirts, floppy-brimmed hats, lace-up boots, and the rest—only all new, of course, not second-hand.*

From the early 1970s, the nostalgia cycle shifted to a smaller cog. Fifties-inspired fashions were swiftly followed by pseudo-mod stylings and the vivisections of punk. In 1978 a garment between ten and twenty years old was reckoned to be *trendy*, with anything older *antique*. The term *vintage* hit its stride during the eighties, taking the place of *antique*—except for garments more than a hundred years old—while *retro* applied to second-hand styles from the past twenty years, as well as made-in-imitations.

Between twenty and thirty years still holds good as

* New jeans have for the past fifty years been given a pre-worn look by bleaching, rips, and simulated signs of wear built into the manufacturing process. For real (not faux-) authenticity off the rack, there are jeans 'worn in' by US prison inmates or, at the top end, by bespoke denim-breakers who wear the daks for six months and get a cut of the selling price.

the lacuna separating contemporary fashion from vintage. Often, though, anything old or ersatz-old will be called *vintage*, never mind that it lacks the prestige and refinement and rarity originally intended by that tag. *Vintage* sells.

And, of course, *vintage* transmutes over time. Just this past couple of years, I've seen op-shopping teens adopt a 'nanna' silhouette—loose-fitting high-waist pants that leave the ankles showing, worn with clumpy shoes and a non-descript puffy top, the whole ensemble glommed in the key of beige. This is vintage as normcore: fashion that purports to be anti-fashion, so drab and wrung-out ironic that it's hard even to mock it. An anti-establishment thread runs back from normcore through Lord Kitchener's Valet to the raccoon-coat craze. To wear a pair of gabardine granny slacks in 2019 is, in its unarresting way, a display of attitude akin to sporting an Edwardian dressing-gown on Kings Road fifty years ago.

But what a comedown from the peacock revolution. *That* was the spirit in which vintage was born, and many still regard vintage and ostentation as inseparable. Before that Edwardian dressing-gown became streetwear, remember, it was good only for fancy dress or theatrical costume. As far back as the 1850s, Henry Mayhew had noted that—

> *Laced coats, and embroidered and lappeted waistcoats, have long disappeared from second-hand traffic—the last stage of fashions—and indeed from all places but court or fancy balls and the theatre.*

Still further back, in 1830s Paris, there had been, among students of a bohemian bent, a short-lived caprice for the 'mediaeval' look. *Fripiers* in Rue de l'École-de-Médicine happily sold them obsolete finery to subvert, since nobody else wanted it. At mid-century, the Pre-Raphaelites' worship of a highly decorative Renaissance sensibility made its mark on fashion, although mainly in interior décor and as reproduction rather than second-hand. A hundred years later there would be Greenwich Village types who, reviving long-dead fashions for a lark, would proclaim themselves 'Beat Pre-Raphaelites'. In between came the Surrealists who, in the words of Susan Sontag, made *le magasin d'occasion* 'a temple of vanguard taste' and the flea market a bourn of 'aesthetic pilgrimage'.

So, from its origins, wearing vintage was essentially performative, and there is that aspect to it still. Historian Jennifer Le Zotte, tracing the progression of second-hand style, takes a tough line on a practice that I'd always seen as harmless—better than harmless in fact, since at its best it gives pleasure to wearer and beholder alike. Le Zotte deprecates what she calls 'vintage exhibitionism' as phoney, elitist and narcissistic, except in the context of queerness. Sure, wearing a garment out of its time and place calls for an amount of play-acting, inhabiting a role as well as a costume. It calls for front, and it *is* a front: a way of standing out *and* a disguise.

Many who buy vintage clothing do so in the spirit of collectors, seeking and cherishing and keeping far more of it than they need. It's not about need. And it's not just about collecting, either. Collectors of vintage think of themselves as custodians—even saviours—treasuring a garment's quality and originality, and thrilled by its survival. Yet vintage is for wearing.

> *When a package at my door contains a dress that another woman wore in 1939, the sense of discovery, of excitement at my acquisition is accompanied by something else: a mysteriously personal union with the past and history.*

And wearing that vintage dress, writes collector and pattern-maker Katalin Lovaśz, makes for a 'bodily engagement' with another time. The satin crêpe fabric of her 1939 dress was cut on the bias, so that its grain, running diagonally, gives a sensuous warp to the garment, a fit and fluidity that's distinctively thirties. A New Look-style dress from the early fifties tells its ungirdled modern-day wearer a very different story. The bodice, tight and unyielding, constricts the ribcage, firm-fitting sleeves are tailored to pin the elbows at a slight bend, while billowing skirts muffle the hips and thighs. Or try a pencil skirt from later that decade, so severely cut as to hobble the stride. Then try a skimpy sixties dress made of stretchy bri-nylon: the fabric may not breathe, but it sure does let you move. If artefacts from the past are the nearest thing we have to time machines, then vintage clothes—intimate, fluent and inhabitable—must count among the nearest of the near.

The playwright Alan Bennett owns a heavy black overcoat more than a hundred years old, 'a lovely thing' with frogging and traces of an astrakhan collar. But what most endears the coat to him is the legend attached to it: that it was made by Proust's tailor. That such a garment should survive to tell its story calls for luck in the long run and quality to begin with. Advocates—not just now but in Mayhew's time, when the shoddy mills were running full pelt—never fail to emphasise the superior quality of old clothes' materials and making. Besides which, as Katalin Lovaśz says, there's 'something subversive about cheating the fashion industry'.

Lovaśz found her 1939 dress on eBay. That's one way of buying vintage. Market stalls and vintage boutiques likewise curate and sell the cream off the top of the second-hand ruck.

But where's the thrill in that? I'm with Ivor Noël Hume, the Indiana Jones of the curio scene in his day, who disdained having his quarry handed him, 'all patched, polished and packaged, with nothing left to do but pay'. When half the thrill lies in the hunt, no place beats an op shop.

CHAPTER 17

Grandad's Clothes

Don't Feed the Moths

FROM A BROTHERHOOD OF ST LAURENCE ADVERTISEMENT, 1974

Op shops were starting to proliferate in Australia by the mid-1970s, as were charity shops and thrift shops elsewhere. The off-piste fashion movement that had grown out of Kings Road and the Summer of Love was partly responsible, as was the revving-up of throwaway culture (and the abundance of stuff to throw away). But even small local charities were beginning to put fundraising on a more businesslike footing. Compared to the 'campaign' approach of an annual jumble sale, an op shop provided a steady income—with donated goods accepted and sold year-round—and gave regular employment to a volunteer workforce ('a wonderful opportunity for housewives with time on their hands'). The shop served as a collection-point for donations and put a face on the charitable body. Our suburb's first op shop, raising money for a local disability-support group, opened in 1974 in a cul-de-sac off the neighbourhood shopping strip.

The Brotherhood of St Laurence, that same year, opened its tenth shop, thirty-seven years after its first. Some of its outlets were rough-and-ready affairs; others, branded Brotherhood Bazaars, were pitched up-market and sold a more select strain of goods, not merely second-hand but 'pre-loved'. Like Goodwill in America, Oxfam in Britain and the Salvation Army everywhere, the Brotherhood ran charitable salvage on a large scale. For years, its salvage operation had relied mainly on sorting and treating rags to sell to industry. It had run regular rag drives, putting 'Brotherhood bags' in letterboxes all through the suburbs and collecting them when filled. And it wasn't just rags and clothing: the Brotherhood would send a van to collect 'anything you do not require', and donations from outlying areas were carried free by the railways. Over time, more and more of the stuff donated was of better-than-rag quality and went to Brotherhood shops for resale.

Fundraising for programs to address social disadvantage

had always been the main goal of the Brotherhood's salvage work. But by the mid-1970s, its objectives would broaden to include 'recycl[ing] goods back into the community, rather than creating new or even false market needs'. In 1977 the first Brotherhood Bins were installed at service stations and supermarket carparks around suburban Melbourne—

> *Now you don't have to wait for us to come and pick up your donation. Instead of leaving it out, cluttering up the porch, you clear it out of the way immediately. Just pop it all straight in one of our bins…*

Not only did the streamlined collection process save the Brotherhood the cost of 'trucking around', but the volume of donations soared, thanks to the bins' convenience—and the anonymity of using them.

In the UK, the proliferation of charity shops knelled the end of the traditional old-clothes trade, vestiges of which had clung on in places like Cutler Street, in London's former Rag Fair district. Charity shops would go main-street and mainstream during the eighties. Rising generations were largely untroubled by the old stigmas linking second-hand with shame and disease. Charity shops were respectable yet non-judgmental, and their flourishing state, in 1980, was said to reflect 'a consciously democratic society'.

Growing affluence, as we've seen, means more things discarded and op/charity/thrift shops have boomed in the decades characterised by ever more and cheaper stuff. As I write, there are close to 2,500 op shops in Australia: nearly every town and suburb has at least one. At a time when buying new has never been so affordable, second-hand consumption is more widespread than at any time since before the industrial revolution.

The big names in op shops—in Australia, the Salvos and Vinnies are the biggest—are trying to reach market segments still resistant to buying second-hand. By hiring paid staff, fitting out stores to more closely resemble mainstream retail, setting higher prices, opening boutiques and pop-ups to sell the choicest stuff, and even stocking some lines of *new* merchandise, they hope to eliminate any lingering associations with the plague-pit. But there's a question still, in some minds at least, as to whom op shops *ought* to be for.

A good deal of contention on the subject surfaced a couple of years ago in a discussion thread on a community Facebook page in the town where I live. Arising from a gripe about the price being asked for a fur coat in one of our local op shops, the thread drew (as such threads do) impassioned comments, initially about prices—*clueless! outrageous!*—then taking on op shops' broader remit—

DP: Op Shops seem to be changing their business models, probably in recognition that a lot of well off people hit the op shops...

KM: Op shops aren't opportunity shops anymore for the less fortunate, they're only vintage shops disguising themselves as op shops.

DP: Absolutely true, but is that the fault of the op shops or the new upmarket customers that now frequent them?

JM: I used to be [a] little angry when I saw people who could quite obviously shop in Target or elsewhere shopping at the op shop. Then I was told how it actually works. Now I understand that the money raised on clothes is actually used for food and other things that the less fortunate may need. I'm now more understanding and accepting that people who actually have money are buying clothes that I and others have donated.

Anxieties and resentments about charitable salvage efforts have never been far from the surface. A press report from 1910 condemned Salvation Army collectors who 'cadge for cast-off clothes and old furniture from well-to-do people in the suburbs, and sell them to the poor'. The writer suspected that '"the poor", as often as not, are second-hand dealers, who sell the goods again at a profit'.

It's entirely possible that collectors misrepresented the use to which donated goods would be put, donors preferring to think that their cast-offs would go directly to the needy, rather than that someone besides the needy might benefit from their sale. Yet the salvage activities of the Salvos and the rest were, right from the start, more concerned with providing the poor with work, shelter and the means to live than with handouts and cheap second-hand. And they never made a secret of it. The Salvos and Goodwill trumpeted the employment and housing programs made possible by their salvage work, and here's the Brotherhood of St Laurence, calling for donations in 1974—

> *All those old clothes are only cluttering your cupboards and feeding the moths. They could be feeding, clothing and housing the less fortunate people of our communities.*

To complicate the picture, nowadays not all op shops are run to benefit a charitable cause. Some, like Savers (and Value Village in the US), are for-profit enterprises. Increasingly, charities are paid a fee for the use of their name on donation bins, but cede the collection, sorting, sale and profits to a commercial player. Which is fine, though you might wish for a little more transparency. Commercially run outfits tend to misrepresent their philanthropic credentials and obfuscate their for-profit status. But, really, who cares? In their anxiety to be rid of unwanted stuff, donors are less likely than they once were to ask who benefits. The same goes for buyers: what matters is that the stock is cheap and hip—and, as a rule, an eye sharpened to profit ensures that less of what's un-hip finds its way onto racks in for-profit stores.

Historian Jennifer Le Zotte condemns the wearing of second-hand *by choice* as 'elective poverty', an expression of class privilege and cultural appropriation.

> *It satisfies a desire to be seen as different than the average consumer dupe, as willing to invest time in the cultivation of originality, supposedly without utilising class and wealth privilege.*

That view is both borne out and bent back on itself by Macklemore's *Thrift Shop*. The song, which topped the *Billboard* and Triple J charts in 2012, saw a white rapper extolling the anti-capitalist, non-conformist cred of thrift-shopping, in pointed contrast to the more characteristic hip-hop aggrandisement of brand names and bling.

But the plaid shirt, velour tracksuit and slippers treasured by Macklemore rank high, to others, among the things that put op shops beyond the pale. For instance, when Englishman Barney Shaw, on an olfactory tour of his local high street, poked his nose into a charity shop, 'The smell of ageing books and ageing people, and the knowledge that both the books and their owners were dead, blended into one melancholy experience.' Most of what you'll find in an op shop nowadays is near-new, cast off by people still living. But there *is* dead people's stuff among it, it's true: I've bought dresses with names like Gladys and Pearl ironed inside the collars, as well as bags of used clothes pegs, hankies softened by wear, Sunday-school prize books, even a set of lower dentures. What draws me to such objects is the palpability of their past lives. Vanessa Berry, herself a passionate op-shopper, has written that she 'mistrusts' new things, preferring second-hand ones 'because they have already had a life before me, and thus seem more human'. I get that. The patina of age.

In the best op shops, stock arrives at random. No racks of same-same-same, but a promiscuous assortment offering no end of scope for surprises. And mystery, as with the item—there's always one—whose function isn't readily apparent. Ask the person behind the counter and like as not she'll reply that she's waiting for a customer to enlighten *her*. Whatever it is, chances are someone will buy it for its beauty or novelty alone. Where else, outside of nature, can you have an experience so uncurated?

Built on amateurism, op shops bring together enthusiasts—sellers and buyers alike—who revel in the unpredictability of the enterprise. It saddens me to see them finessed by creeping corporatism: the gloss put on and the chance taken out. But it's funny. For perhaps a hundred years, successive generations of curio-hunters have worried that, one day soon, all the good stuff would dry up. It hasn't yet. You've just got to keep looking.

CHAPTER 18

Trash and Treasure

'Why not flog it in the Trading Post?*'*

GRAHAM KENNEDY, *IN MELBOURNE TONIGHT* ON GTV-9, C.1966

Caribbean Gardens opened on Melbourne's outer suburban fringe in 1965. It combined ornamental gardens with attractions like train rides and mini-golf, all set around a lake originally made for speedboat-testing. From early on, as an extra drawcard, a car-boot sale was held there on Sundays. Beginning with just a handful of vendors, the Caribbean Gardens Sunday market grew, by the late-seventies, to be huge and has stayed that way. But a Sunday market now isn't what a Sunday market was. Fresh produce, plants, crafts, twice-removed bric-à-brac, and curated vintage predominate now, where once people sold mainly their own unwanted stuff.

How else was a suburban household to dispose of its surplus before there were charity bins and op shops in every suburb? They could send it to the tip, dump it in a creek, or, in the case of cumbersome items, for a designated period each year leave them out on the nature strip to be carted away as 'hard rubbish'. Paradise for scavengers! A 1950s-model fridge, painted red, appeared kerbside the same week I moved out of home and kept on humming for ten years. (It's humming still, for all I know.)

Trash and treasure markets, which took off in Australia in the 1970s, followed the American trend of flea markets, which took *their* lead, in name if not exactly in spirit, from the original flea market, *le marché aux puces*. It had been born, you may recall, in the shake-out of Paris's 1883 rubbish-bin ordnance, which curtailed the livelihood of the *chiffoniers*, or rag-pickers. Displaced from their traditional quarter of the city, the waste-sellers—not just rag-pickers, but others of the scavenging trades classed as *les pêcheurs de lune* (moon-fishermen)—congregated in the suburbs, forming a 'market with fleas'.

The spread of chain grocery stores offering the convenience of one-stop shopping would eventually undermine the viability of urban marketplaces. Second-hand stalls, in many cases, filled the gaps left by fresh-produce vendors, changing the markets' character. In the US, 'flea market' was the name given to those that came to trade predominantly in second-hand. In the 1960s and '70s, drive-in movie theatres would start running weekly flea markets to make up for lost revenue as TV stole their audiences and daylight saving ate into showtimes. On Sundays, before seven-day trading became the norm, suburban shopping malls might also host markets in their vast, empty carparks. This was the trash and treasure wave caught by Caribbean Gardens. Stall hire was cheap, overheads non-existent and anyone with a card table and beach umbrella, or just an open car-boot, could set up to sell their own stuff.

Or else there was the garage sale—otherwise known as a yard sale, porch sale, lawn sale, tag sale, sidewalk sale or stoop sale. Originating in the US in the 1950s, the garage sale was a means of culling a household's superseded appliances and furniture—an accumulation that reflected the 240 per cent increase, nationwide, in annual spending on such goods between 1945 and 1960. Garage sales were a way, too, for housewives to make some money. Women had long been the entrepreneurial force behind rummage sales; now they put those skills to work for their own benefit. (The earliest private garage sales were actually called rummage sales.)

Just a generation earlier, it would have been unthinkable for a woman to invite neighbours and strangers to pick over and buy her old things. What had changed? Tupperware and Avon, it's true, had begun to normalise commerce in the home and between female friends. But whither the old shame of second-hand? Being based on surfeit rather than want, the garage sale seemed to count as a wholesome expression of suburban striving, even a form of neighbourliness. Selling implied a boast of having upgraded—to a bigger TV, then a colour one—while buying entailed the virtue of a bargain.

Like flea markets, garage sales went stratospheric in the 1970s, becoming not just a suburban pastime but an off-the-books industry. In the US, by the end of that decade, it was worth nearly a billion dollars a year, tax-free. Garage sales now have far more than neighbourhood appeal. Dealers and collectors come early and make a rapid sweep, exquisitely attuned to the items they seek, yet blind to the lure of the crockpot or Totem Tennis. In some places, garage sales are regulated. Local authorities in the US charge as much as $75 for a permit; in Australia, no such charges apply, though residents of one Melbourne municipality require an Excess Garage Sales permit to hold more than three per year. There are garage sales where a whole street or even whole town gets in on the act. The World's Longest Yard Sale, held annually, stretches for more than a thousand kilometres through six states along US Route 127, and since 2011 the Australia-wide Garage Sale Trail has promoted re-use by coordinating thousands of garage sales across one weekend each spring.*

Garage sales are the bane of the op shop. Not because they're the competition, but because, late any Saturday afternoon, the unsold—unsaleable—residue of innumerable garage sales will be stuffed into charity bins and dumped outside op shop doors. There are garage-sale protocols that frown on op shop dumping, and on plastering the neighbourhood with flapping flyers. Taped to every pole and post, those flyers are often cagey about the precise address of the sale. 'Signs out at 8 a.m.,' they might say, followed by the bold-print injunction: NO EARLY BIRDS. But there always *will* be early birds, prowling the neighbourhood from daybreak, looking for signs of activity and—the giveaway—balloons.

Garage sale early birds tend to get lumped in with the 'crawlers' who pick over the hard waste left out for kerbside collection. (Like me with that red fridge—but I *rescued* it!) Some householders get a bit touchy about people taking their stuff, although legally, once it's outside their fence line, it no longer *is* theirs. It belongs to the council

* For a laugh, google 'How to Avoid Possessed Items at Garage Sales'.

or the collection contractor, who generally turn a blind eye to the virtuous tradition of crawling. After all, re-use is preferable to landfill, and courteous crawlers observe the niceties: leaving the pile tidy, and never breaking a set by taking just one chair.* To be possessive of your cast-off stuff is, by one reckoning, 'kind of being un-Australian'.

Not so long ago, nothing could have been *more* Australian than to buy and sell second-hand goods through the *Trading Post*. Launched in Melbourne in 1966, the *Trading Post* was a newspaper filled with classified listings of items for sale, modelled on similar publications in the US, with a nod to the pioneering *Exchange and Mart*. It began as a free paper with a small suburban distribution but found a wider audience after the TV host Graham Kennedy plugged it on his popular variety show, *In Melbourne Tonight*. When a contestant was less than overjoyed with a prize they won on his spinning wheel, Kennedy would say, 'Why not flog it in the *Trading Post*?' For three decades or more—first in Victoria, then nationally—the newspaper was the go-to forum for buying and selling anything you could think of, from a car to a camera† to...a pair of jousting sticks.

* I'd like to see a protocol mandating that any brown lounge suite left out be torched. But that's just me.

† I bought a compact Rollei camera through the *Trading Post* to take travelling in 1985.

The *Trading Post* had a cameo role in the 1997 film *The Castle* as the bible of the Kerrigan family. Young Steve Kerrigan pored over each week's issue and, spotting a promising item—an overhead projector, say, or those jousting sticks—would consult Darryl, his father and haggling coach. Whatever the asking price, Darryl invariably scoffed, 'He's *dreamin'*.'

Within ten years of that high-water mark the print edition of the *Trading Post* had all but lost its market to online platforms such as eBay and Gumtree: its last issue ran in 2009. eBay originated in 1995 as AuctionWeb, a free sales site that soon changed name and began to charge listing fees. Its international reach, shop-from-home convenience and secure, regulated transactions gave eBay an immediate edge over traditional buy-and-sell forums. Gumtree and Craigslist, on the other hand, owe their success to the attributes they share with garage sales and the old-style *Trading Post.* Despite operating online, they have a neighbourhood flavour. Buyers can search for items in their locality, contact the seller by phone ('Tell him he's *dreamin'*') and pick-up is often preferred. And yes, there are jousting sticks.

Used and vintage clothing sales thrive on eBay. I went there recently for a lethal Edwardian hatpin and could, with just a few more keystrokes, have found the hat, frock, boots and brolly—the full suffragette kit—to go with it. Specialist clothing resale platforms include Poshmark and ThredUp, where, much like traditional consignment boutiques, vendors curate and sell pre-loved quality fashion for prices somewhere between new and thrift shop.

If second-hand has become more respectable, some of the credit must go to eBay. In a poll conducted by eBay in 2008, seventy per cent of adult respondents felt that buying used goods was more socially acceptable than it had been five to ten years earlier. It can still be a leap, though, for someone accustomed to buying at a digital remove to venture into an op shop. Even if it doesn't smell of death, your average op shop manifests that element of randomness which is the mother of serendipity. The online universe of searchable, white-glove second-hand has its uses. But it is mighty bloodless.

Garage sales are less common now than ten years ago. Redundant household appliances, exercise machines, and drum kits tend to be posted straight to Gumtree or on local Facebook groups. Prams and other baby gear, in particular, are typically sold or gifted within social networks, or, just as commonly, sent straight to an op shop as the most frictionless means of divestment.

But a garage sale is still practically inescapable when it comes to moving house or handling a deceased estate. Approached in the right spirit (Everything Must Go) nothing reduces the overburden like a clearing sale. The other option is storage—but what begins as an interim measure can easily become indefinite, and storage doesn't come cheap. Defaulting on the rent of a storage unit will result, in due course, in the contents being auctioned off, sight unseen. Long-running reality TV shows have been built around the suspense and avarice—gambling, really—that attend the storage auction. Truly, it's second-hand at its seediest.

In the US, a franchise advertising itself as 'the caring alternative to traditional junk removal' aims to find new homes for unwanted furniture. For a fee, Junkluggers won't just cart away a customer's old lounge suite, but will offer it to three thrift stores before consigning it to either landfill or auction. Should one of the thrift stores accept it, a tax-deductible receipt is issued to the donor, offsetting Junkluggers' fee. It's a small gesture towards keeping usable goods in circulation.

When an elderly family member dies, there may be little of value left behind (other than sentimental value, and maybe not even that). To vacate a property, sometimes the entire contents will be scooped up holus-bolus and presented to the nearest op shop, hence the used pegs and hankies, the bath salts and lavender bags and half-empty bottles of 4711 you sometimes find. There are second-hand dealers, too, who offer comprehensive 'deceased estate management' services. In preparation for a property sale, they'll clear out the house and shed, take care of the cleaning and gardening, and keep as their fee 'your unwanted assets' for resale.

My mother was a child of the Depression. She says that's why she finds it difficult to part with things and her every drawer and cupboard bulges with stuff. Plus, she volunteers in an op shop, so she's always accumulating more. Though she tries to practise 'get one, get rid of one', it doesn't always work. Mum knows she has too much stuff and hates the idea of being a nuisance, even posthumously. She says to me, often, 'I don't want you to have to deal with all this.' The residue of a loved one's life can cause distress, annoyance—and guilt. One woman, left her late parents' accumulations to 'deal with', summed up the experience like this—

> *You start off by wanting them to have good homes, all the things that are left over from another person's life, and then you end up by saying, 'Oh, let's just get rid of them.'*

CHAPTER 19

The Belly of a Shark

'New-new open, new-new open, bend down select...'

SECOND-HAND TRADER'S PATTER,
KARIMO MARKET, NIGERIA, 2014

'Let's just get rid of them'? Easier said than done.

The world and its op shops are swamped with cheaply produced and easily shed goods—clothing, homewares, toys, you name it—as well as the casualties of technological change, often in the shape of books. Over the past twenty years, China's industrialisation and economic engagement have brought down the price of many if not most goods. At the same time, fashion has picked up speed.

Across the globe during the 1990s and 2000s import

quotas on textiles were relaxed as part of the liberalisation of markets. Imports from low-wage countries were far cheaper than garments manufactured locally in places like Europe, America and Australia: people could afford to buy more of them, and they did. While clothing prices fell by more than twenty per cent, consumption rose by as much as a third. But it wasn't just about affordability. The internet, along with innovations in production and supply chains, made it easier than ever to stimulate and satisfy consumer desires. Traditionally, new fashions would be released each season—summer, autumn, winter, spring. Now, mass-market clothiers like Zara and H&M can introduce new short-run fashion lines every few weeks.

A cheap garment produced by the fast-fashion complex may not be made to last, but it will almost certainly outlive the fleeting trend it was meant to embody. With replacement far outpacing dilapidation, the result is 'fashion pollution'.

Clothes aren't just cheaper than they were twenty years ago, they're cheaper than they've ever been. In 2014, clothing cost American households, in real terms, roughly a quarter what it had in 1901. Individuals were on average devoting the smallest percentage of income ever to their clothes. Yet, amazingly, people have never bought and owned as many garments as they do now. Per capita, Australians buy new clothes amounting to more than double the global average; only an American buys more. An estimated sixty per cent of an Australian woman's wardrobe is inactive: each garment is worn, on average, just seven times before being retired. Under-thirty-fives are quick to get rid of any garment whose fashion moment is past: by selling it online, sending it to landfill or even burning it. Their parents and grandparents wear—or at least keep—their clothes for longer (never quite long enough to be in fashion again) and are more likely to give them away to charity.

Or at least to deposit them in a donation bin, which is not always the same thing. In fact, donation bins are cogs in the worldwide apparatus of waste recycling. More than a third of Australia's ten thousand-odd donation bins are operated by commercial textile merchants, to whom a sizeable proportion of clothing given direct to charities is also channelled. Garments unsold by op shops or judged unsuitable for sale will be sold, by weight, to textile recyclers.

Most charities work in partnership with commercial operators. In the UK, however, the international charity Oxfam runs not just an extensive network of charity shops but also its own textile-processing offshoot, Wastesaver. More than seventy per cent of clothing donated to Oxfam ends up at the Wastesaver plant, to be sorted and graded for export or recycling, or as waste. In this way, Oxfam maximises both the value of its donations and the integrity of its humanitarian mission.

Most donors nowadays are inured to the idea that their cast-off clothing may benefit a business rather than a cause. With unwanted clothing piling up like never before, ease of disposal is a key consideration. It's hard now to conceive of the ruckus that ensued in 1976 when a British newspaper exposé revealed that Children's Research Fund donation bins were run by a commercial operator that returned just twenty per cent of the profits to the charity. It was dubbed the Great Charity Clothing Scandal—but that's pretty much standard operating procedure today, with most charities receiving either a flat fee or anywhere from five to fifty per cent of profits from textiles siphoned to their commercial partners.

You can't blame the charities. Most of them began collecting unwanted goods intending to benefit their cause from sales through volunteer-run op shops. Instead, they found themselves in the waste-management business. There must always have been a percentage of donations that were no better than rubbish, but in recent years Australian charities have had to pay millions of dollars annually for waste-collection. They blame the cheapness and surfeit of consumer goods—furniture and appliances that cost less to replace than to repair—and donors' unwillingness to take responsibility for their own waste.* Especially though, they blame fast fashion.

'Fast fashion has no intrinsic value in the fibres; it's not designed to last,' says the National Association of Charitable Recycling Organisations (NACRO), the Australian peak body whose very name spells out what op-shop charities have become. While the quantity of clothing donations has soared, the quality has plummeted. And though fast fashion has obsolescence built in—fabrics quickly tear and pill, seams split, hems unravel, buttons come loose, zips fail—that doesn't mean it's easily disposed of. Apart from the smothering abundance of it, there's the cockroachy persistence of its elements, leaking greenhouse gases and shedding plastic microfibre as they ever so slowly degrade.

That's if the clothing is sent to landfill. The big op-shop charities do their best to redirect what they can't sell to recyclers instead. There's still a huge and lucrative market for wiping rags, used by industry and the auto trade. Or clothing may be shredded into flock, as of yore, for use in mattresses, seating, carpet underlay, insulation, even acoustic speakers. Until recently, the Indian city of Panipat, not far from Delhi, dominated the world shoddy trade, recycling woollen garments into blankets for use

* Notwithstanding the elevation of decluttering to a form of spiritual purification.

in disaster-relief operations. Less than a decade ago, Panipat produced 100,000 blankets a day and supplied ninety per cent of relief-blankets worldwide. Now, China can produce polar fleece blankets, lightweight, bright-coloured and brand-new, almost as cheaply as Panipat's shoddy ones. The recycle potential of old woollens has all but vanished. Not so cashmere. Upscale fashion labels tout *regenerated* cashmere, made of *post-consumer* (that is, second-hand) yarn 'painstakingly' pulped and re-spun in Italian shoddy mills. Sustainability being a monetisable virtue, garments advertised as 'Cashmere with a Conscience' don't come cheap. And, of course, nobody calls it shoddy.

Fabric blends such as cotton-polyester pose a problem when it comes to recycling, just as their predecessors did in the nineteenth century. And scientists, just like *their* predecessors, are seeking chemical processes that will efficiently separate a fabric's constituent fibres—even its dyes—leaving each available for re-use. Polyester, if sent to landfill, leaks chemicals for decades; if separated out it can be re-used multiple times, in progressively lower-grade products. Likewise cotton which, left to rot, emits carbon dioxide.

Worldwide, it's estimated that seventy-three per cent of discarded clothing is landfilled—or incinerated. Not only are cast-off clothes among the fuel that replaces coal in some 'green energy' plants, but it's not uncommon for individuals to burn unwanted garments. A 2017 Australian survey found—'disturbingly'—that almost one in ten millennial respondents got rid of clothes by burning them. It may be surprising in a modern context (where on earth do they build the pyre?), but it's a mode of disposal as old as the naked flame.

In times long past, Japanese monks might burn the garments of the dead in a ritual meant to clothe those reborn as wandering ghosts. Such a ritual was held to blame for the *furisode kaji* (or 'swinging sleeves fire') of 1657 which, according to legend, began with a burning robe at a temple, spread when it was caught by a strong wind and killed an estimated one hundred thousand citizens of Edo (modern-day Tokyo). In India, gold-embroidered saris, once past wearing, are burnt to retrieve the precious metal. Closer to home, in an era before charity bins and environmental by-laws, a bonfire was the usual postscript to a jumble sale. Foremost among the items fuelling the blaze were women's hats. In an age of comparatively slow fashion, nothing dated as fast as a hat. 'Hats go for about seven a penny, don't they?' asked a helper pricing goods for a sale in 1903. Ahead of a jumble sale in 1950, the vicar appealed to donors: 'Please don't send any hats.' More than a thousand had been sent in for the previous year's sale and most had ended up as fuel for the church boilers—though, even in that capacity, they'd proved less than satisfactory.

Looking to the future, there are brave hopes that fashion upcycling—creating new garments from old—will catch on as a mainstream trend, or even that mass-market brands might develop subscription-based fashion rental as a more sustainable way to satisfy consumers' appetite for change. In the meantime, of the fifty-plus million tonnes of new clothing produced worldwide each year, it is estimated that only a single-digit percentage will live on as second-hand. That may sound negligible, but it translates to second-hand clothing in the millions of tonnes per year: far more than can be absorbed by the voracious first-hand markets here in the Global North.* And so it gets sent to sea, most of it, bound for the Global South.

ෆ

Africa has long been on the receiving end of cast-off clothes. Remember all the police uniforms and livery Britain sent south in the nineteenth century as a sop to the colonised? Under a 'Peace and Friendship' treaty dating from 1786 that granted US exporters unfettered access, Morocco was, for more than a hundred years, a

* It seems strange that Australia should be classed as part of the Global North; but that's now the preferred term for what used to be called 'the developed world' or 'first-world countries'.

prime destination for America's unwanted second-hand. African markets were deluged with surplus military gear after both world wars and, as the twentieth century wore on, the provision of used clothing would be a component of any international response to famine, war or disaster.

What opened the floodgates for the second-hand trade to Africa, though, was the economic liberalisation regime advanced by the World Bank and International Monetary Fund during the 1980s. Tariffs and household incomes fell in affected countries across sub-Saharan Africa, creating markets ripe for cheap imports. Unable to compete, local textile and garment industries languished and were eclipsed by the used clothing trade.

In the twenty years after 1980, the world trade in used clothing increased, by volume, around seven-fold; then a further *ten-fold* since the turn of the century. By value, the trade grew at almost double the rate of the new-clothing industry in the decade to 2016, a period during which sales of new clothing skyrocketed as prices plunged. The US, UK and Germany are the three biggest exporters, but in 2016/17 Australian exports of 'worn textiles' (rags as well as clothing) approached 100,000 tonnes, bound for Asia and the Pacific, as well as for Africa.

It's hard to get an exact picture of how much of the world's second-hand ends up in Africa. Of the more than seventy per cent of used clothing that goes unsold domestically by British charities and textile recyclers, for instance, a large portion is sent to places like Pakistan and Ukraine for processing and on-shipping. But United Nations figures show that in 2016, sub-Saharan Africa absorbed around one-fifth* of the world's used clothing, more than any other region. Kenya alone imported about 100,000 tonnes. Even ten years earlier, about one in every six containers shipped to Africa from the US was filled with used clothing.

Used clothing—collected by textile recyclers either straight from donation bins or as unsold stock from op shops—is sorted and graded and wrapped tightly in bales weighing 45 kg (100 pounds) each. Usually it's the second-cut of garments that go to Africa; the first-grade might be sold elsewhere in the Global North, to South or Central America, or to Asia, with the lowest grades destined for countries in Central Asia. Garments are baled according to type (women's tops, men's trousers, T-shirts) as well as by fabric, winter garments being diverted from the Africa trade. It takes about 550 bales to fill a forty-foot shipping container, which will likely be carried as cheap 'back-freight' in a ship that has unloaded a valuable cargo and might otherwise return to Africa almost empty.

Many who donate their old clothes are surprised to

* Other sources put that share at closer to one-third.

learn that second-hand clothing judged unsaleable in the Global North is (except in the case of humanitarian relief, and even then…) sent to Africa not as charity, but *for sale.* The containers shipped by textile merchants are bought by African importers, from whom wholesalers buy bales by the score, which they sell in ones and twos to second-hand traders, who sell direct to the public. There's money to be made at every point in the process, not just by those doing the selling, but by customs agents, border officials, market inspectors and government authorities large and small.

It's believed that as many as eighty per cent of Africans rely, either solely or in part, on clothes bought second-hand. With most traders selling from market and roadside stalls, the extent of the industry is hard to map. What's certain is that it provides a livelihood—albeit often a meagre one—to some hundreds of thousands across the continent. Alongside the sellers, there's a thriving side-industry in mending and alterations.

Choosing a bale at the warehouse is a gamble. Bales are sold to dealers 'blind'—still sealed and bound, labelled only (and sometimes misleadingly) as to what type of clothing they contain. A Lagos warehouse inventory includes the following categories: 'Children Mix, Original shorts, Men trousers, Men Polo/T Shirt, Ladies Tops mix, Ladies dress mix, Boys Trouser, Ladies Bra, Ladies

Trouser'. Bales of underwear, children's clothing, skirts and jeans are the most sought after and highly priced. Branding on some bales—Goodwill (US) or Salvos stores (Australia)—may hint at their origins, but there's no telling the quality and condition of what's inside. One damp or dirty garment can contaminate the entire bale; or perhaps the contents were second rate to begin with, or unpopular sizes preponderate. A run of such unlucky bales can put a trader out of business.

With a new bale to sell, a market trader puts the word around that there's to be an 'opening day'. When a bale is cut open in front of them, customers consider its contents to be 'new'—not already picked over and denuded of all the choice items. Wrinkled garments, hung up fresh from the bale, have market-place cachet; if laundered and ironed, they are suspected of being 'third-hand'—that is, of having already been worn and cast off locally. The opening of a bale may even be staged as an exclusive event, with customers paying for the privilege of first pick. Whatever the setting, customers thrill to see a bale's plastic strapping sliced through and the wrapping spring open. They flock around, bending down to select from the garments spilling out on the ground. At the Karimo Market in the Nigerian city of Abuja, the traders' enticing patter is non-stop: 'New-new open, new-new open, bend down select, small-small money.'

Bend down select (or just *ben daun*) is one of the names used clothing is called by in Nigeria. In Zambia, it's *salaula*, Bemba for 'to rummage through a pile'; in Congo-Brazzaville it's *sola* (to choose); in Kenya and Tanzania *mitumba* (bundles); and Rwandans say *chagua*, Kiswahi'li for 'to select'. Another common naming thread can be seen in *obroni wewu* ('white man's deads'—Ghana), *Kafa ulaya* ('the clothes of the dead whites' or 'died in Europe'—Kenya and Tanzania), and *Marehumu* George ('the late George'—also from Kenya). Those names seem to have been adopted in the 1960s and '70s, when used clothing from the West was still a novelty in African marketplaces. Locals reasoned, says Ghanaian writer Nana Kofi Acquah, that the garments must have belonged to people who had died, since 'no one in their right mind would willingly give away such nice articles'.* To Mozambicans, who were introduced to second-hand clothing as humanitarian aid when their country was torn by civil war in the 1980s, it's still *roupa da calamidade*, 'clothing of calamity'. Zimbabweans call it (with what degree of irony, I can't say) *mupedzanhamo*, 'where all problems end'.

Nigeria is Africa's most populous nation and its biggest market for used clothing. The country has its

* Acquah is known for his writing and photography capturing Accra's Kantamanto Market—see http://africaphotographer.blogspot.com/2013/02/dead-white-folks-stuff-in-accra.html

own expansive lexicon for the trade—besides 'bend down', there's 'fairly used', *gbanjo, bo si corner, wo o wo, toks,* and 'London clothes'—but *okrika* is how it's best known.* Okrika is the name of a port in south-east Nigeria, through which slaves were once traded. In colonial times cast-off clothing came through Okrika in the form of missionary welfare packages. Even after a new port eclipsed theirs early in the twentieth century, Okrika people continued ferrying goods to the markets upriver. And so, explains Okrika-born 'Ibime', 'when second-hand clothes are landing, *okrika* is on its way'.

Although up to eighty per cent of the used clothing shipped to West Africa ends up for sale in Nigeria, its importation to that country has been banned since the 1970s. Officially, the ban was introduced to protect the local textile industry, but some believe that, after the civil war (1967–70), the government was seeking to punish Igbo people from the secessionist south-east, who dominated the *okrika* trade. The country's western neighbours Benin and Togo, which have populations around five per cent of Nigeria's but no import restrictions, receive through their ports more used clothing than could ever

* *Gbanjo* is Yoruba for 'cheap' or 'bargain', *bo si corner* means 'go [in]to a corner', *wo o wo* is 'try it on' (traders in *new* clothes being reluctant to let buyers try them on), and *toks* is short for *tokumboh*, meaning 'from overseas'. *Okrika* is shortened, especially by students, to *ok*.

be absorbed within their own borders. In fact, importing goods banned by Nigeria is a mainstay of neighbouring economies and smuggling across the country's 'porous' borders is epidemic. Profiling Lagos's roaring *okrika* scene in 2016, journalist Cyriacus Nnaji mugged, 'How the second-hand clothes got into the Nigerian market remains one of the greatest mysteries of mankind.' From time to time, a customs bust will get wide coverage, as when thirty-seven bales of contraband clothing were found hidden under cow dung in the back of a truck not far from the border with Benin in 2017. Mostly though, bribes ensure that *okrika* passes undetected through checkpoints on its way to Nigerian markets.

In 2015, *News Ghana* journalist Gubemi God's Covenant Snr pushed his way through 'a massive explosion of human beings' at the Katankowa *okrika* market, Lagos's biggest. 'It was,' he said, 'like being caught in the belly of a shark.' Even when they didn't have a bale freshly opened, most of the three thousand-odd traders displayed their stock in heaps on the ground for customers to bend down and rummage through. At Aswani Market ('where Lagosians worship at the shrine of second-hand clothes'), Cyriacus Nnaji wrote:

> *Capricious young men and women ring bells and shout, '50, 50 Naira, 100, 100 Naira, 200, 200 Naira, bend down select, select your own, na*

> *mungu dedo boutique!' The customers cause a huge stampede, as women, most especially, fall over one another in order to make their choices.*

The same scene plays out on a smaller scale at stalls by roadsides and busy bus stops all over the city and countryside.

Overlaying the market's crush and clamour is the pervasive odour of unwashed *okrika*—not, as you might suppose, the reek of stale sweat, but rather of the chemicals (disinfectant? pesticide?) with which bales are treated prior to shipping. Only as, with maturity, he became aware of the distinctly different smell of new clothing did Olumide Abimbola realise the extent to which *okrika* is 'sewn into the imagination of everyday Nigerians'.

Four East African countries—Kenya, Rwanda, Tanzania and Uganda—in 2015 announced their intention to phase out second-hand clothing imports in order to stimulate local textile industries. By increasing tariffs, they hoped to render the trade unviable by 2019. US textile merchants protested that constriction of the second-hand trade with East Africa would result in the loss of forty thousand American jobs. (The value of US exports to the region had peaked in 2012 at US$43 million.) In response, the US Government threatened in 2017 to suspend the four African countries from a trade agreement that, for almost twenty years, had allowed them to export commodities such as coffee, tea and textiles to the US, free of tariffs or import quotas. 'This is not Free or Fair Trade,' tweeted President Trump, 'it is Stupid Trade.' The East African countries backed down on their proposed ban. But Rwanda had already imposed a steep tariff increase on used clothing imports—up from twenty US cents to a prohibitive US$2.50 per kilogram—which had the effect of a ban and which it refused to repeal.

Rwanda's government was emboldened by a 'Made in Africa' initiative, backed by Chinese companies keen to set up garment factories in the region. 'African countries,' says the initiative's official spin, 'can benefit from the relocation of 85 million jobs from China to jumpstart their economic transformation.' Another way to view it is that, with labour costs in China rising, Africa is being eyed as the next source of cheap labour: global fast fashion's new factory floor.

For its part, Rwanda's government saw an opportunity to rebuild domestic industries and a skilled workforce, and for Rwandans to take pride in wearing new locally made clothing rather than imported cast-offs. 'In China during the 1980s there were also a lot of people wearing old, second-hand clothing,' said Candy Ma, co-owner of a flagship garment factory in the capital, Kigali. 'I think that for a country's civilisation to progress you do need to stop that.'*

With tariffs now so high, imports of used clothing into Rwanda have predictably slowed to a trickle. Officially. It's expected that *chagua* will continue to find its way in from neighbouring countries, just as *okrika* does in Nigeria. Customers will pay more and the government will miss out on tariffs. With locally made new garments typically costing four times more than the second-hand article, though, few Rwandans can afford to buy them. Cheap imports from China will offer the next-best option should supplies of *chagua* flag. In fact, according to the American development agency USAID, it's not second-hand but the prospect of high-volume imports of new clothing from China that poses the greatest threat to rebuilding textile industries in Africa.

Beyond all that lies a question: do African customers *prefer* new clothes? Doubtless some do; but, amid the rarefied talk of dignity and independence, voices from the marketplace beg to differ. 'The new clothes are like uniforms,' scoffed a young man wearing a rhinestone-studded shirt at a second-hand shop in Kigali. 'It

* Several African governments have run scare campaigns linking second-hand clothing to diseases including thrush, scabies, tinea, syphilis, gonorrhoea, genital warts, chicken pox and hepatitis, as well as with infestation by parasites. For reasons of hygiene, Ghana banned the sale of used underwear in 2011.

looks bad, like we are a sports team or a group of church singers.' Another shopper, at Ogbeogonogo Market in Asaba, Nigeria, insisted 'that people, especially children, look smarter and cute in these bend down stuffs than new ones'.

Some 'bend-down boutiques' really are boutiques: shops rather than market stalls; no bending down necessary. A trader with an eye for choice items in the marketplace or who pays a premium for first pick from new bales, then washes and displays their stock on racks, might attract a more affluent clientele. One Lagos *okrika* wholesaler advertised top-grade 'London Bales', as well as brand items sold by the piece—'All items directly from London, Super AAA Quality (Boutique grade), not the junk people send to Africa.'

There's a saying among second-hand traders in Nigeria: '*Okrika* isn't only for the poor.' Indeed, 'Gentlemen and ladies park classy cars to buy these fairly used clothes,' and a survey of high-income households in the Zambian capital, Lusaka, found that around two-thirds sourced most of their clothes as *salaula*. For some, it's true, there's shame attached to wearing second-hand. A university student 'scouting for choice bum-shorts and beautiful tops' among a bale of *okrika* at the Karimo market in Nigeria's capital, Abuja, confessed that only her close family knows that her clothes are 'fairly used'.

But outweighing the shame is pride, and even prestige, in finding quality clothes that look better than what's available new.

Traders at Lagos's Katankowa market felt sure that durability, more than price, accounts for *okrika*'s cross-class appeal. A buyer bending down at an open bale told a local journalist, 'It is a lot of prudence to buy these fairly used clothes because, in the long run, they are stronger and cheaper than the new ones.' Some affluent customers justify their recourse to second-hand by pointing out that many brand-name items sold new—especially jeans and sneakers—are, in fact, cheap knock-offs, while those sold used are the real thing. Mindful of that, a switched-on market trader might, by subjecting counterfeit Nikes or Levi's to scuffing and traces of wear, pass them off as prized authentic second-hand.

At an asylum-seeker safe house in the US in 2017, a Rwandan refugee named Allan oversaw a stock of donated second-hand clothing. Of all those who passed through, he said, it was the Congolese men who had the best eye for style. The cities of Brazzaville and Kinshasa, on facing banks of the Congo River, have long been home to *La Société des Ambianceurs et des Personnes Élégantes* (the Society of Ambiance-makers and Elegant People), or *La Sape*. Gold-trimmed liveries and other gaudy European cast-offs, used by colonisers to reward and curry favour with their African subjects, bred in these two Congolese cities a cultural movement of radical dandies or *sapeurs*. *La Sape* lives on, more flamboyant than ever, though the modern *sapeur* craves bespoke or designer finery over second-hand.

For most traders, selling used clothing returns a meagre but—barring a run of bad bales—dependable living. One trader at Biryogo Market, in Kigali's Muslim quarter, has sold *chagua* for more than thirty years, supporting herself and five children. USAID estimates that throughout East Africa the industry employs more than 350,000 people, earning US$230 million annually. There are concerns about widespread loss of livelihood in countries like Rwanda where the industry is under threat, and that those displaced from the male-dominated trade will encroach on women's jobs in other industries.

From either side of the market stall, second-hand counts as a significant and—why not?—legitimate industry and an indispensable part of life. British writer Andrew Brooks, in his book *Clothing Poverty*, pitched the African used-clothing trade as a dark morality tale. But then, it was Brooks who also put the view (in 2015!) that 'The purchasing of pre-consumed used clothing at charity shops, thrift stores and yard sales is perceived negatively as undesirable, acceptable only for the impoverished and countercultural groups in Western society.'

While Brooks is among those who seem determined to associate used clothing with victimhood and taboo, I guess I'm predisposed to associate it with choice. Here in the Global North, as in sub-Saharan Africa, the popularity of second-hand cannot now and never could be explained by economics alone.

CHAPTER 20

...Under the Sun

When I thought of *Nothing New* as a title, I didn't know how right it was. Only as the book took shape did I come to see how the history of second-hand borrows from and reinhabits itself, over and over. The reader will feel by now that they can practically hum the tune. And yet, there's novelty, an original turn, to be found at every stage.

Have I dwelt too much on what second-hand offers and too little on what it denies?

My resort to second-hand is a choice, it's true, stemming not from need but from an ideology that favours improvisation over aspiration. I can see how, to someone for whom new isn't an option, second-hand could be a demeaning, despicable thing. But it doesn't have to be. Now more than ever, second-hand presents plenty of possibilities to up-end such antiquated notions as *seedy* or *down at heel* or *disreputable*.

What's more, for the bargain-hunter second-hand is brag-worthy. There are people for whom *nothing new* amounts to a badge of honour. 'These jeans? Five bucks!' Or, 'Everything I'm wearing comes from an op shop.' Or, furnishing a home (even building one): 'We picked it all up second-hand.'

For good or ill, though, second-hand comes with baggage, be it nostalgia, moth holes, traces of wear or the stink of condescension and squalor. Second-hand isn't for everyone. But—let me theorise—the capacity of second-hand to repel or attract depends more on the beholder than the beheld.

My hunch is that a taste for second-hand goes along with a tolerance for dirt. It's long been acknowledged that dirt is relative, 'a thing in the wrong place' as an old saying has it. (The allusion, originally, was to the alchemical nature of manure.) The same goes for trash and treasure: 'One person's trash…' et cetera.

Just so, dust—

The dust comes secretly day by day,
Lies on my ledge and dulls my shining things.
But o this dust that I shall drive away
Is flowers and Kings,
*Is Solomon's temple, poets, Nineveh.**

Not just a patina, but the actual stuff of age and dilapidation. And—oh joy, oh woe—there is no end to it.

* Viola Meynell, 'Dusting'. The poem appears in *The Week-End Book* (1924), a treasure-trove of songs, recipes, natural history and parlour games, edited by Meynell's brother Francis and bought by me second-hand.

ACKNOWLEDGMENTS

Thanks to:

Linda Notley for generously responding to my appeal for library catalogue cards, an ever-scarcer commodity that I use for note-taking. Adele Walsh and Kelly Gardiner put out the call on their *Unladylike* podcast.

Michele O'Brien, Social Policy Library Manager at the Brotherhood of St Laurence, for her help with accessing BSL op shop and recycling history.

Christine Whelan and James Whelan of Kartaway, for showing me over their transfer station so I could see for myself that there's no such thing as waste.

The good folk at the Anglican op shop in Holbrook, NSW, who opened up specially one Saturday afternoon so I could buy that pair of jodhpurs.

David Bannear for a million things, hardly any of them second-hand.

SOURCES

It's only fitting that this books draws on facts, stories, words and ideas that came to me second-hand. Other writers have rummaged through and around this subject before me, and their work helped shape this one. A list of suggested further reading can be found at the end of the book.

I'm especially indebted to the unbylined journalists whose writings live on in digitised newspapers online. Trove Newspapers, hosted by the National Library of Australia, yields more treasure than any jumble sale—and for free.

What follows will guide readers to some of the source materials I drew on, chapter by chapter. Anyone seeking more complete information is welcome to contact me: mrsbradley@robynannear.com

INTRODUCTION

p. 4 *one British academic* —Andrew Brooks on p. 8 of his book *Clothing Poverty: The Hidden World of Fast Fashion and Second-hand Clothes* (see Further Reading).

p. 9 The quote from Margaret Atwood's novel *Lady Oracle* (first published in 1976) is from the 2009 Virago Press edition, p. 192.

p. 10 *the costliest garments, the bravest panoplies* —George Augustus Sala's *Twice Around the Clock, or The Hours of the Day and Night in London* (Houlston & Wright, London, 1859), p. 169.

Unattributed quotes in the early chapters come from volumes 1 and 2 of Henry Mayhew's opus, *London Labour and the London Poor* (see Further Reading).

1: NOTHING NEW

Helpful to me in writing this and the next chapter were: Madeleine Ginsburg, 'Rags to Riches: the second-hand clothes trade 1700–1978' (*Costume* 14, 1980); Laurence Fontaine, 'The Exchange of Second-hand Goods between Survival Strategies and "Business" in Eighteenth-Century Paris', in Fontaine (ed.), *Alternative Exchange* (see Further Reading); Beverly Lemire, 'Consumerism in Preindustrial and Early Industrial England: The Trade in Secondhand Clothes' (*Journal of British Studies*, vol. 27, no. 1, 1988).

James Boswell quotes are from his *London Journal, 1762–1763* (William Heinemann, London, 1950), pp. 109 & 115.

2: OL' CLO'

Charles Dickens quotes are from 'Meditations in Monmouth-Street' (*Morning Chronicle*, 1836), later included in *Sketches by Boz*.

p. 23 *There are many parts of the metropolis…* —James Grant, *Lights and Shadows of London Life* (Saunders & Otley, London, 1842), p. 121.

p. 25 *from a wooden leg to an orrery* —'The Jewerie of London', *Jewish Herald* (Melbourne), 22 Oct. 1880.

p. 26 *many cast-off clothes allowed them…* —*Launceston Advertiser* (Tasmania), 18 July 1833.

p. 28 *a man's third-best coat…* —Andrew Wynter, 'Old Clo'', in *Our Social Bees* (second series, Robert Hardwicke, London, 1866), p. 272 —first published in *Cassell's Family Paper*, 1865.

p. 30 *householders in small-town America were warned…* —*Janesville Gazette* (Wisconsin), 16 June 1855.

p. 33 *a preparation of dirt…* —Wynter (as previous), p. 278.

p. 34 *But let the wearer beware the first shower…* —John Thomson & Adolphe Smith, *Street Life in London* (Sampson Low, Marston, Searle & Rivington, London, 1877), p. 33.

p. 35 *down the scale respectable* —Thomson & Smith, pp. 48–9.

p. 38 *There seems to be some popular belief or superstition…* —*Argus* (Melbourne), 2 Jan. 1877, p. 6.

p. 38 *The red coat is held in the highest estimation...* —*Watchman and Wesleyan Advertiser* (London), 19 Nov. 1862, p. 5.

p. 40 *for a year or two after, scarcely a carter...* —*Sydney Gazette and NSW Advertiser*, 25 Feb. 1836, p. 4.

p. 43 *This little fib...* —Wynter (as previous), p. 273.

3: THE WAIFS AND STRAYS OF CIVILISATION

Quotes on the subject of pawnbroking in Ireland come from Appendix E to the 'First Report of Commissioners for Inquiring into the Condition of the Poorer Classes in Ireland', also known as the Poor Laws (Ireland) Commission, 1836. You can find this vivid document online.

p. 48 *a London pawnbroker will often lend more...* —Sala (as previous), p. 171.

p. 55 *a black doll in a white frock...* —Dickens, 'Meditations in Monmouth-Street'.

4: NO SUCH THING AS WASTE I: THE HUMBLE RAG

p. 63 *on every unoccupied piece of land*—*Ovens and Murray Advertiser* (Beechworth, Victoria), 19 Nov. 1873, p. 2.

p. 64 *The* Deseret News *failed to appear...* —'Affairs in Utah', *New York Times*, 10 Aug. 1861, p. 4.

p. 68 *a preparation of wool made from thrice-worn...* —Wynter, p. 278.

p. 68 *is now returned to us, after paying two freights...* —*Ballarat Star* (Victoria), 29 April 1886, p. 2.

p. 68 *the people who purchase it...* —*Queanbeyan Age* (NSW), 8 July 1886, p. 4.

p. 69 *Fashions used to last a lifetime...* —Thomson & Smith (as previous), pp. 48–9.

p. 70 *The cloth is not really bad...* —*Argus* (Melbourne), 2 Jan. 1877, p. 6.

pp. 70–71 *No man can say that the materials...* and *Thus, the final destination...* —*Sydney Morning Herald*, 20 Jan. 1865, p. 2 —quoting *The Times* (London).

p. 73 *No attempt at cleansing or disinfecting...* —*Tocsin* (Melbourne), 22 Sept. 1904, p. 3.

p. 74 *You mothers of girls...* —*Leader* (Melbourne), 24 July 1915, p. 51.

5: NO SUCH THING AS WASTE 2: THE INSATIATE BAG OF THE WASTE COLLECTOR

I learned much about *chiffoniers* and the garbage regimen in Third Republic Paris from Alaine Faure's 'Sordid Class, Dangerous Class? Observations on Parisian Ragpickers and their *Cités* During the Nineteenth Century' (*International Review of Social History,* no. 41, 1996), pp. 157–76 (translated by Lee Mitzman).

p. 77 *The principle which guides him…* —*Australian Star* (Sydney), 8 June 1907, p. 8.

p. 85 *by night and by day…* —*Letters and Papers, Foreign and Domestic, of the Reign of Henry VIII,* 5 Nov. 1538, vol. 13, part 2, ed. James Gairdner (London, 1893), p. 757.

p. 85 *the great national quarry* —Donald Woodward, 'Swords into Ploughshares: Recycling in Pre-Industrial England' (*Economic History Review,* vol. 38, no. 2, May 1985), p. 180.

p. 88 *It needs almost the subtle eye…* —*Australian Star* (Sydney), 8 June 1907, p. 8.

6: DESTITUTE OF APPAREL

p. 91 *Could not some means be adopted…* —in a letter to the *South Australian Weekly Chronicle,* 5 Sept. 1885, p. 5.

p. 92 *I ask you whether any observant person…* —*Mercury* (Hobart), 9 Oct. 1865, p. 2, quoting a report from an English newspaper.

p. 94 The inner-city missionary was my great-great-great-grandfather John Cromack; his journals are in the Melbourne City Mission collection at the University of Melbourne Archives.

p. 94 *As the apparel of these poor people…* —*Morning Post* (London), 20 Oct. 1852, p. 1.

p. 95 *It is only a common act of Christian charity…* —*South Australian Register,* 3 July 1852, p. 7.

p. 96 *Your old housekeeper will be seriously vexed…* —*Goulburn Herald* (NSW), 3 Aug. 1867, p. 8.

p. 97 *in our modern times…* —*Australian Star* (Sydney), 11 Oct. 1894, p. 9.

p. 98 *There is a great deal of poverty and distress…* —*Horsham Times* (Victoria), 26 Sept. 1894, p. 4.

p. 98 *Any description of left-off clothing…* —*North Melbourne Gazette,* 10 June 1898, p. 3.

p. 100 Margaret Bale/Martin Able's story was related in Perth's *Sunday Times*, 7 Aug. 1910, p. 3.

p. 101 *Cast-off clothing for the women of the bush!...* —*Sunday Times* (Perth), 1 Nov. 1914, p. 7.

p. 102 *obtrude on the mind of the recipient...* —*Australasian* (Melbourne), 12 July 1879, p. 6.

p. 102 *'Can you tell me,' asked ...* —*Australian Women's Weekly*, 9 May 1936, p. 19.

p. 104 Michael Harrington, *The Other America: Poverty in the United States* (Macmillan, New York, 1962), p. 5.

7: HER SUPERFLUOUS FAL-LALS

p. 106 *Women such as this...* —Louis Sébastien Mercer, *Tableau de Paris*, 1781 (trans. Helen Simpson: Lippincott, Philadelphia, 1933), p. 392.

p. 107 *no lady likes to be caught...* and *a shrewd old Frenchwoman* —*Indianapolis Journal*, 11 Jan. 1873, p. 2, quoting the *New York Mercury*.

p. 107 *To wear a dress out...* —'100-guinea gowns. What becomes of them?', *Fremantle Mail* (Western Australia), 16 June 1905, p. 4.

p. 107–08 *The "ol' clo'" lady is now no old nagging harridan...* —*Capricornian* (Rockhampton), 5 April 1902, p. 5.

p. 108 *It is a boon to the woman who is obliged...* —*Fremantle Mail,* 1905 (as previous).

p. 108 *precautions are taken...* —*Evening News* (Sydney), 10 Sept. 1905, p. 7.

p. 109 *It is an unwritten law among them...* —*Age* (Melbourne), 23 May 1906, p. 13.

p. 110 *in such a way, however, that they do not know...* —*Newcastle Herald* (NSW), 22 Feb. 1913, p. 4.

p. 113–14 Press commentary on the sale of Mary Todd Lincoln's First Lady wardrobe is quoted from *Behind the Scenes, or, Thirty Years a Slave, and Four Years in the White House* by Elizabeth Keckley (G. W. Carleton, New York, 1868).

8: ENOUGH HUMILITY TO WEAR A RUMMAGE HAT

p. 118 *The peculiarity of the Rummage Sale...* —*Middlesex Courier*, 31 July 1891, p. 6.

p. 119 *When the doors were opened...* and *Although advertised to be held...* —*Middlesex Courier*, 16 Oct. 1891, p. 6 and 29 July 1892, p. 3.

p. 120 *When one sees a crowd of ill-clad women...* —*Age* (Melbourne), 20 May 1924, p. 6.

p. 120 *mothers save up for months...* —*Leader* (Melbourne), 13 April 1918, p. 45.

p. 121 'The Success of Our Rummage Sale' by Sydney Phelps was syndicated in newspapers all over Australia in 1903, as was Mary Stewart Cutting's 'The Mother of Emily', in 1905.

p. 123 *the Sydney free kindergarten's jumble sale...* —*Sydney Morning Herald*, 15 April 1908, p. 5.

p. 124 *pathetic of countenance...* —*Age* (Melbourne), 20 May 1924, p. 6.

p. 125 *Many and awesome...* and *Clothing of all kinds...* —*Register* (Adelaide), 24 March 1927, p. 31.

p. 126 *Who has not heard wife or husband say...* —*Geelong Advertiser* (Victoria), 15 Oct. 1917, p. 3.

p. 126 *the quaint comb bought in Colombo...* —*Australasian* (Melbourne), 27 April 1918, p. 25.

p. 127 *I would have liked to buy it...* —quoted by Alan Attwood, *Age* (Melbourne), 27 Jan. 1979.

9: SILVER SHOES FOR SIXPENCE

Two books in particular helped clarify the origins of charitable salvage efforts by the Salvation Army, St Vincent de Paul's and Goodwill: Susan Strasser's *Waste and Want: A Social History of Trash* (see Further Reading); and *Charity Shops: retailing, consumption and society* by Suzanne Horne and Avril Maddrell (Routledge, London, 2012).

p. 139 *The Opportunity Shop in aid of the YWCA Hostel...* —*Geelong Advertiser* (Victoria), 22 Sept. 1927, p. 4.

p. 142 *An instructive inventory of the passé...* —Mary McCarthy, *The Group*, Weidenfeld & Nicholson, London, 1963, p. 278.

p. 143 *hundreds of women of the working-class* —*Sydney Morning Herald*, 24 April 1921, p. 5.

p. 143 *dingy and cramped little shop* —*BSL Notes*, April 1957.

p. 144 *police had to control the crowds pressing around* —*BSL Volunteers Newsletter*, 14 Aug. 1981.

10: FOUND

The stand-out source for this chapter was William FitzGerald's 1895 article for *Strand* magazine (see Further Reading).

p. 145 *Because we do not know if they were lost or stolen...* —Nadja Spiegelman, 'The Peculiar Poetry of Paris's Lost and Found', 10 Sept. 2017, https://www.newyorker.com/culture/culture-desk/the-peculiar-poetry-of-pariss-lost-and-found [Ax March 2018].

p. 150 *It does not occur to the officer that the presence of a tortoise...* —*Argus* (Melbourne), 14 Nov. 1908, p. 7.

p. 150 *the change of attire often takes place...* —*Western Australian*, 26 Oct. 1929, p. 16.

p. 151 *unhallowed by association...*; *two of the most powerful impulses...* —*Argus* 1908 (as previous).

p. 153 *for some strange reason, shirts* —*Argus* (Melbourne), 25 June 1904, p. 17.

p. 154 *no man may know...* —*Argus*, 1908 (as previous).

p. 154 *A simmer of laughter...* —*Argus*, 1904 (as previous).

p. 155 *a few needles stuck in a cork*; *simply devoured by curiosity...* —*Australasian* (Melbourne), 27 June 1908, p. 48.

11: OPEN TO OFFERS

Heidi Egginton's terrific article 'In Quest of the Antique' (see Further Reading) provided valuable background for this and the next chapter on the heyday of *Exchange and Mart* and the *Bazaar*.

p. 159 *Acting upon [the] well-known and lamentable weakness...* —*Leader* (Melbourne), 19 March 1870, p. 5.

p. 160 *among ladies of the less well-to-do order...* —*Argus* (Melbourne), 3 April 1869, p. 5.

12: THE ANTIQUARIAN THICKET

p. 167 *extended self* and *passion for possession* —Anna Catalani & Yupin Chung, 'Vintage or Fashion Clothes? An investigation inside the issues of collecting and marketing second-hand clothes' (paper presented at the 8th International Conference on Arts and Cultural Management, Montréal, Canada, July 2005), pp. 3–4 —http://neumann.hec.ca/aimac2005/PDF_Text/CatalinaA_ChungY.pdf [Ax April 2017].

p. 167 *antiquities that he never looked at...* —Ivor Noël Hume,

Treasure in the Thames (Frederick Muller, London, 1956), pp. 23–4.

p. 168 *The collector is always waiting…*; *Collecting is a way of linking…* —William Davies King, *Collections of Nothing* (University of Chicago Press, 2008).

pp. 168 & 174 Nicolas Bentley quotes are from 'a recent BBC talk' quoted in *Northern Times* (Carnarvon, Western Australia), 3 May 1951, p. 5.

pp. 172 & 175 William Plomer's poem 'Caledonian Market' appeared in the *Spectator*, 5 April 1940, p. 14 —http://archive.spectator.co.uk/article/5th-april-1940/14/caledonian-market [Ax March 2018].

p. 172 *ordered showrooms* —*Bazaar*, 29 Oct. 1927, p. 470.

p. 173 *old and beautiful* —Heidi Egginton, 'In Quest of the Antique' (see Further Reading), p. 1.

p. 173 *a deeply held need for enchantment…* —Egginton, p. 12.

p. 173 *the charm of useless knowledge…*; *took pleasure in dates…* —George Orwell in *New Statesman*, 17 Aug. 1940.

p. 174 *queer sort of person…* —'Sydney Topics', *Age* (Melbourne), 11 July 1933, p. 9.

p. 174 *the attitude of an heir* —Walter Benjamin, 'Unpacking my Library', 1931 (trans. Harry Zohn).

p. 174 Joseph Mitchell's collection was detailed, with photos, by Paul Maliszewski in 'The Collector', *Granta 88*, Winter 2004, pp. 151–92.

13: A CURIOUS TRINKET

p. 179 *mystery crates* —*Telegraph* (Brisbane), 14 March 1946, p. 5.

p. 183 *Recent finds in op shops and garage sales…* — Steven Morris, 'Work attributed to Andy Warhol, aged 11, to go on show in UK', *Guardian*, 10 May 2012 —www.theguardian.com/artanddesign/2012/may/10/andy-warhol-aged-11; Stacy Conradt, '8 Amazing Garage Sale Finds', mentalfloss.com, 8 Aug. 2011 —http://mentalfloss.com/article/28457/8-amazing-garage-sale-finds; 'James Cockington, '$4 op shop buy sells for $75,000, *Sydney Morning Herald*, 25 June 2013 —www.smh.com.au/money/investing/4-op-shop-buy-sells-for-75-000-20130625-2otj4.html [all Ax Sept. 2018].

p. 185 *Nosing one day in the dust laden shelves* and *It was merely a curiosity…* —Gregory M. Mathews, 'My Life Story' (unpublished manuscript), National Library of Australia, MS 1134.

p. 186 *like a junk shop —all over the place —Age* (Melbourne), 14 Feb. 1950, p. 16.

p. 186 *It was so full of stuff...* —Adrien A. Browne's shop, in *Sun* (Sydney), 2 June 1946, p. 7.

14: STEEL SALAD

This chapter draws on insights salvaged from Adam Minter's *Junkyard Planet: Travels in the Billion-Dollar Trash Trade* and Bernard Jullien's essay on the history of the second-hand car market, in *Alternative Exchanges* (ed. Fontaine). (See Further Reading.)

p. 189 *you wander through long avenues... —Daily Mercury* (Mackay, Queensland), 19 May 1939, p. 9.

p. 190 *This immense relic weighs 1,340 pounds... —Norfolk Virginian* (Virginia, USA), 8 Oct. 1867.

p. 191 *Huge electrical transformers jostle ships' boilers... —Daily Mercury* (Mackay), 1939 (as previous).

p. 192 *shrewd benignity —Camperdown Chronicle* (Victoria), 24 Oct. 1940, p. 4.

p. 192 For the full story of Jack Peacock and Dudley Flats, see David Sornig's *Blue Lake: Finding Dudley Flats and the West Melbourne Swamp* (Scribe, Melbourne, 2018).

p. 195 *in the corner of a junk shop —West Australian*, 6 March 1934, p. 12.

p. 195 *Mudguards hang from the ceiling...where appearance is discounted...When he wants to repair the roof...* —*Sun* (Sydney), 14 Aug. 1927, p. 23.

15: MENDING VS ENDING

I learned much about thrift and its enemies from *Waste and Want: A Social History of Trash* by Susan Strasser (see Further Reading).

p. 201–02 Léon Werth quotes are from *33 Days*, (Melville House, New York & London, 2015), translated by Austin Denis Johnston.

p. 203 *The shoes once worn by a WAAF... —Daily News* (Perth), 12 Jan. 1944, p. 4.

p. 203 *buttons and badges should be removed... —Geelong Advertiser* (Victoria), 16 June 1919, p. 2.

p. 206 *hardly a farm... —Albany Advertiser* (Western Australia), 15 July 1940, p. 3.

p. 206 *One room…is devoted to a heterogeneous mass…* —*Barrier Daily Truth* (Broken Hill), 11 Aug. 1941, p. 5.

p. 206 *The father and mother of all junk shops* —*Argus* (Melbourne), 1 March 1946, p. 10.

p. 207 *their present wardrobes will not be made obsolete…* —Strasser, p. 231, quoting a 1942 US War Production Board press release.

p. 209 *The thrifty mother undoes a bundle…* —*Evening News* (Sydney), 19 Sept. 1905, p. 7.

p. 210 *spend too much time on old garments* —*Harper's Household Book* (New York, 1913), p. 108.

p. 210 *premeditated poverty* —Emily Holt, *The Complete Housekeeper* (Doubleday, 1917).

p. 212 *from the shackles of tradition…* —Roy Sheldon & Egmont Arens, *Consumer Engineering: A New Technique for Prosperity* (Harper, New York, 1932).

p. 212 *Wearing things out does not produce prosperity…* —Earnest Elmo Calkins in *Consumer Engineering* (see previous), pp. 1–2.

p. 213 *Basic utility cannot be the foundation…* —B. Earl Puckett, quoted in *Time* magazine, 3 July 1950.

p. 214 *The more the rhythm of purchase exceeds the rhythm of dilapidation…* —Roland Barthes, *The Fashion System*, Hill & Wang, New York, 1983, p. 298.

16: WHAT DID YOU WEAR IN 1969, GRANDMAMA?

p. 218 The Salzmans and their raccoon coats were the subject of a 'Talk of the Town' piece in the *New Yorker*, 17 Aug. 1957, pp. 20–2.

p. 224 Susan Sontag quotes come from *On Photography* (Farrar, Strauss & Giroux, New York, 1973), p. 54.

p. 225 *When a package at my door contains…* and *something subversive…* —Katalin Lovaśz, 'Playing Dress-up: eBay's Vintage Clothing-Land', in Hillis, Petis & Epley (eds), *Everyday eBay: Culture, Collecting and Desire* (Routledge, New York, 2006), pp. 283–5.

p. 226 The story of Alan Bennett's overcoat comes from *Keeping On Keeping On*, p. 141, and *London Review of Books*, 4 Jan. 2018, p. 39.

17: GRANDAD'S CLOTHES

Brotherhood of St Laurence publications (*Brotherhood News, Brotherhood*

Action, BSL Notes) quoted in this chapter have been digitised and are available (by arrangement) in the library at BSL headquarters in Fitzroy.

p. 231 *a consciously democratic society* —Madeleine Ginsburg, 'Rags to Riches' (as previous), p. 133.

p. 235 *It satisfies a desire to be seen as different…* —Jennifer Le Zotte, *From Goodwill to Grunge*, p. 243. (See Further Reading.)

p. 236 *The smell of ageing books and ageing people…* —Barney Shaw, *The Smell of Fresh Rain* (Icon Books, London, 2017), p. 89.

p. 236 Vanessa Berry is quoted from her zine *Vinnies* (1999) —https://vanessaberryworld.wordpress.com/zines/ [Ax Sept. 2017].

18: TRASH AND TREASURE

On the origins of flea markets and garage sales, two books were especially helpful: *Waste and Want* by Susan Strasser and *From Goodwill to Grunge* by Jennifer Le Zotte. (See Further Reading.)

p. 244 *kind of being un-Australian* —Chris Jager, 'Is it Illegal to Take Other People's Junk During Council Cleanups?' www.lifehacker.com.au/2015/04/ask-lh-is-it-illegal-to-take-other-peoples-junk-during-council-cleanups/ [Ax Sept. 2018].

p. 248 *You start off by wanting them to have good homes…* —Ellen, an interviewee quoted by Jackie Goode in her essay 'Moving On: Overlooked Aspects of Modern Collecting', *Alternative Exchanges* (ed. Fontaine, see Further Reading), p. 178.

19: THE BELLY OF A SHARK

For this chapter I drew on an abundance of (shifting) facts and figures as well as on reporting by journalists in Africa and elsewhere. The following helped me to get a grasp on the international trade in textile recycling: Andrew Brooks, *Clothing Poverty* (see Further Reading); Karen Tranberg Hansen, 'Charity, Commerce, Consumption: the International Second-hand Clothing Trade at the Turn of the Millennium—Focus on Zambia' —in *Alternative Exchanges* (ed. Fontaine, see Further Reading); Political economist and social anthropologist Dr Olumide Abimbola, blogging as loomnie, 6 May 2009 —https://savageminds.org/2009/05/06/consuming-second-hand-clothing/ [Ax Dec. 2017]; Shannon Brady and Sheng Lu, 'Why is the used clothing trade such a hot-button issue?', 2 Aug. 2018 —www.just-style.com/analysis/why-is-the-used-clothing-trade-such-a-hot-button-issue_id134132.aspx [Ax Sept. 2018]; Natalie L.

Hoang, 'Clothes Minded: An analysis of the effects of donating second-hand clothing to sub-Saharan Africa', BA thesis, Scripps College (USA), 2015 —https://scholarship.claremont.edu/scripps_theses/671/ [Ax Sept. 2018].

p. 255 The 'disturbing' trend of burning one's unwanted clothes was among the findings of a YouGov Omnibus survey widely reported in the Australian press on 6 Dec. 2017.

p. 260 *New-new open, new-new open, bend down select…* —quoted by Angeleen Nkwocha in the *Authority* (Lagos) Oct. 2014 —www.authorityngr.com/2014/10/Karimo-Okrika-Market-where-the-rich-and-poor-meet.html/ [Ax Dec. 2017].

p. 262 *when second-hand clothes are landing,* okrika *is on its way* —'Ibime', in discussion thread: 'Why are Second-hand Clothes called Okrika in Nigeria?', June 2013 —www.nairaland/com/1322011/why-second-hand-clothes-called-okrika [Ax Dec. 2017].

p. 266 *The new clothes are like uniforms…* —a market customer quoted by Lily Kuo, writing for *Quartz Africa*, 29 Nov. 2016 —https://qz.com/661463/a-chinese-garment-factory-is-helping-rwanda-wean-itself-from-western-hand-me-downs/ [Ax July 2018].

p. 267 *people, especially children…* —quoted by Kennedy Bienose, 'Second-Hand Clothes: The Boom, Gains and Pains', *Pointer* (Delta State, Nigeria), 29 June 2017 —http://thepointernewsonline.com/?p=26594 [Ax Dec. 2017].

p. 267 Okrika *isn't only for the poor*—quoted by John Thomas Didymus, 6 April 2012 —www.digitaljournal.com/article/322488 [Ax Dec. 2017].

p. 267 *Gentlemen and ladies park classy cars* —Dupe Olaoye-Osinkolu ('Duposh'), 30 Nov. 2016 —www.smartviewsmagazine.com/features/okrika-clothes-pocket-friendly-health-challenging/ [Ax Dec. 2017].

p. 267 *scouting for choice bum-shorts…* —Angeleen Nkwocha in the *Authority*, 2014 (as previous).

p. 268 *It is a lot of prudence to buy these fairly used clothes* —customer quoted by Kennedy Bienose in *Pointer* (as previous).

FURTHER READING

Henry Mayhew, *London Labour and the London Poor; A cyclopaedia of the conditions and earnings of those that will work, those that cannot work, and those that will not work*, published in four volumes, 1851–62.

Of most interest to me in writing this book were volumes 1 and 2: The London Street Folk. All four volumes in their entirety can be found online, digitised by Project Gutenberg or the Internet Archive.

Jennifer Le Zotte, *From Goodwill to Grunge: A History of Secondhand Styles and Alternative Economies*, University of North Carolina Press, Chapel Hill, 2017.

Laurence Fontaine (ed.), *Alternative Exchanges: Second-hand Circulations from the Sixteenth Century to the Present*, Berghahn Books, New York, 2008.

Andrew Brooks, *Clothing Poverty: The Hidden World of Fast Fashion and Second-hand Clothes*, Zed Books, London, 2015.

Susan Strasser, *Waste and Want: A Social History of Trash*, Metropolitan Books, New York, 1999.

Adam Minter, *Junkyard Planet: Travels in the Billion-Dollar Trash Trade*, Bloomsbury Press, New York, 2013.

The author, himself the product of a junkyard dynasty, chases the garbage across continents and oceans to find out where our unwanted stuff ends up. An eye-opening read, especially in light of the ongoing landfill and recycling crisis.

Ivor Noël Hume, *All the Best Rubbish*, Harper, New York, 1974 (reissued 2009).

A classic appreciation of finding and collecting, by an antiquarian turned archaeologist.

Ted Sandling, *London in Fragments: A mudlark's treasures*, Frances Lincoln, London, 2016.

This book by a modern-day mudlark is illustrated by photos of small treasures plucked from the Thames at low tide.

Heidi Egginton, 'In Quest of the Antique: *The Bazaar, Exchange and Mart* and the Democratization of Collecting, 1926–42' —in *Twentieth Century British History*, November 2016, pp. 1–27.

Egginton really gets the allure of collecting and second-hand, unlike most academic writers who approach the subject as ethnography. Find her article online at —https://academic.oup.com/tcbh/article/28/2/159/2571307 [Ax July 2019].

William G. FitzGerald, 'The Lost Property Office', *Strand* magazine, vol. X, July–December 1895, pp. 641–53.

Featuring eye-popping photos taken inside the lost property depots of the major railway stations and Scotland Yard, this article is a real gem. You can find it, digitised by the Internet Archive, at —

https://archive.org/stream/TheStrandMagazine AnIllustratedMonthly/TheStrandMagazine1895bVol.XJul-dec#page/n651/mode/2up [Ax July 2019].